A
NEW SCIENCE of
THE PARANORMAL

D1306489

Other Books

by Lawrence LeShan

The Psychosomatic Aspects of Neoplastic Disease (coedited with David Kissen)

Counseling the Dying (with Margaretta K. Bowers, Edgar N. Jackson, and James A. Knight)

Towards a General Theory of the Paranormal (mongraph)

The Medium, the Mystic, and the Physicist

How to Meditate

Alternate Realities

You Can Fight for Your Life: Emotional Factors in the Development of Cancer

Einstein's Space and Van Gogh's Sky (with Henry Margenau)

The Mechanic and the Gardener: Understanding the Wholistic Revolution in Medicine

The World of the Paranormal: The Next Frontier

Cancer as a Turning Point

The Dilemma of Psychology

The Psychology of War

Meditating to Attain a Healthy Body Weight

Beyond Technique: Bringing Psychotherapy into the Twenty-First Century

An Ethic for the Age of Space: A Touchstone for Conduct among the Stars

Patriotism for Grownups: How to Be a Citizen in the Twenty-First Century (with Eda LeShan)

The Pattern of Evil: Myth, Social Perception, and the Holocaust

The Mallorca Conference on Human Potentialities (with Arthur Twitchell)

A
NEW SCIENCE OF
THE PARANORMAL

THE PROMISE OF PSYCHICAL RESEARCH

Lawrence LeShan, Ph.D.

QUEST
BOOKS

Theosophical Publishing House

Wheaton, Illinois • Chennai, India

First Quest Edition 2009

Quest Books
Theosophical Publishing House
P.O. Box 270
Wheaton, IL 60187–0270

www.questbooks.net

Cover image © 2009 German Ariel Berra, from BigStockPhoto.com
Cover design by Kirsten Hansen Pott

Library of Congress Cataloging-in-Publication Data

A new science of the paranormal: the promise of psychical research / Lawrence LeShan.—1st Quest ed.
    p.   cm.
Includes bibliographical references and index.
ISBN 978-0-8356-0877-0
1. Parapsychology.   I. Title.
BF1031.L435 2009
130—dc22   2008042883

5   4   3   2   1   ★   09   10   11   12   13   14

Printed in the United States of America

To Gertrude Schmeidler, Ph.D.,
who taught so many of us so much about psychical research

What if you slept?
And what if,
In your sleep,
You dreamed?
And what if,
In your dream,
You went to heaven
And there plucked a strange and beautiful flower?
And what if,
When you awoke,
You had that flower in your hand?
Ah, what then?

—Samuel Taylor Coleridge

Humanity has dreamed and has awakened with a strange and beautiful flower in its hands. The flower is the solid and impossible data that psychical research has produced. Now we must face the question. "Ah! What then?"

—Lawrence LeShan

Contents

1

✦

Psychic Research and the Consistency of the Universe

One morning in the late 1960s, three of us were sitting and talking in the New York City headquarters of the Parapsychology Foundation (an organization devoted to the study of paranormal phenomena). There were Martin Ebon, executive director of the foundation; Betha Pontorno, its secretary; and I, who was there under a research grant. Eileen J. Garrett, the foundation's president, came in. She was the premier psychic of the period, a woman of unquestionable integrity who had spent the last fifty years trying to understand the meaning of her mediumship. (She had been analyzed by C. G. Jung in this search and been examined by a wide variety of scientists.) In the 1920s and '30s she had worked extensively in London with a psychic researcher named Hereward Carrington.

Mrs. Garrett greeted us, and we went into her office to discuss the day's work. She told us about a curious dream she had had during the night. She said, "I dreamed Carrington came into my room and told me to take care of his wife, who needed me. He also said that while I was doing this, I should look for a box of very important research papers under the bed that was being ruined by a wallaby sleeping on them."

We then speculated briefly about the meaning of this dream (Carrington had been dead for over twenty years) and then moved on to other matters.

Chapter One

The next morning Mrs. Garrett came in early, called us into her office, and said, "We are in trouble. I know myself. Last night I dreamed Carrington came again into my bedroom, very angry. He said he had told me his wife needed me and I had done nothing about it. He then kicked me out of bed, and I woke up on the floor."

None of us had the faintest idea where Carrington's widow would now be. Our only clue was that she was English; if she was still alive, the best place to start looking for her was in England. We made a list of the leading older psychic researchers in England who might have an inkling where we could find her. Then we each took a part of the list and started telephoning. We reached six or seven of them, and none had the slightest notion where she might be or even if she were still alive. When we came up dry, Mrs. Garrett called someone she knew high up in the tax department of Great Britain. After a good deal of cajoling (to which we all listened on the extensions), we located the last known address. It was (as readers of Agatha Christie have already guessed) a cottage out on the moors in Devon. Mrs. Garrett then called the local police station and said that she had been talking to someone in the area who told her that they had just passed the cottage and that something seemed very wrong there.

A local constable went to the cottage and found Mrs. Carrington. She was in her late eighties. She had fallen three days before and broken a hip, and had been unable to get up. She was on the floor, had soiled herself, had had nothing to eat but an apple, and was in very bad shape. No one was expected to come to the cottage for the next three days. She would probably have been dead by then. They had taken her to a local hospital by ambulance.

When Mrs. Carrington was stabilized, Mrs. Garrett arranged to have her taken to a large hospital in London to be put under the care of a leading physician there whom Eileen had known for many years. We called the Society of Psychical Research in London, and they sent someone out to the cottage. There *was* a box of papers under the bed, but it consisted only of things that should have been thrown out thirty years before, shopping lists, paid gas bills, and so forth. Of a wallaby there was no sign.

A month or so later, when the four of us were again together and talking about the matter, Mrs. Pontorno said, "Mrs. Garrett, please don't have any more dreams like that. The last one cost us £1200."

Here is another example of this kind of event:

In 1930, a one-eyed pilot named Hinchliffe was attempting the first east–west transatlantic flight. He had intended to fly alone. Unexpectedly, at the last moment, his financial sponsor insisted on a woman copilot. Several hundred miles away, on an ocean liner, unaware that Hinchliffe was making the crossing attempt at this time, or that there were any plans for anyone to be with him, two old friends of his, Air Force Colonel Henderson and Squadron Leader Rivers Oldmeadow, were in bed. In the middle of the night, Henderson, in his pajamas, opened the door of Oldmeadow's cabin and said, "God, Rivers, something ghastly has just happened. Hinch has just been in my cabin. Eyepatch and all. It was ghastly. He kept repeating over and over again, 'Hendy, what am I going to do? What am I going to do? I've got the woman with me and I'm lost. I'm lost.' Then he disappeared in front of my eyes. Just disappeared."[1]

It was during that very night that Hinchliffe's plane crashed, and he and the woman copilot were killed.

This is the type of data that historically has been the primary concern of psychical research. The information that Henderson reported was both meaningful and important. Unfortunately, very little progress has been made in the past hundred years to increase our understanding of this type of phenomenon.

It is with the meaning and implications of these occurrences that this book is concerned.

There is a tremendous hope and great promise in psychical research—the study of the paranormal. In spite of where the field appears to be now, this promise is close to fulfillment. We know far more about the paranormal than is generally believed.

This book is about that promise and how we can achieve it. The first chapter is largely concerned with what has held us back. The rest of the book explains how we can go forward.

The scientific study of paranormal phenomena—ESP, poltergeists, hauntings, deathbed apparitions—is in complete disarray. The major laboratories have closed, and scientific journals in the field have shown nothing importantly new for many years. The few libraries dealing with the subject are deserted on an average afternoon, and this at a time when there is tremendous and widespread public interest in the paranormal.

This book tells why this is so. It explains why psychical researchers have abandoned the study of large, well-attested psychic events (examples of which are scattered through the book) and limited themselves largely to studying statistical analyses of people guessing thousands of cards being turned over in the next room or next country, or of people trying to influence by mental means the long lists of numbers produced by an electronic random-number generator. This approach has shown scientifically that ESP exists, but it has been unconvincing to the mainline scientific establishment and, moreover, of little interest to the public at large. The book then proceeds to show how a real science can be made out of the large, exciting events—such as the incidents mentioned at the beginning of this chapter—that brought most of the psychical researchers into the field. If this can be done, it would bring mainline science into the study of psi and thus revitalize the whole field. Our culture would be changed in a positive way as the reality of the paranormal became part of our general worldview and of our concept of what it means to be a human being.

The issues here are far from being merely academic. We desperately need a new concept of what a human being is if we are to learn how to stop killing each other and poisoning our only planet. The old, materialistic worldview has not enabled us to do this. Psychic research, however, does offer the opportunity for a new picture of the world. That is what this book is all about—that, and the way to go to build the new worldview and have it generally accepted.

A major conflict has been going on in philosophy for nearly three thousand years. It is over the question of how many *kinds* of things there are in reality. It may well have started in the sixth century B.C. with the Milesian Presocratic philosophers such as Thales and Anaximander. They contended that everything was basically composed of one substance. (Thales said it was water; Anaximander said it was the *apeiron*, the "boundless"). Thus everything in reality obeyed the same laws and could be explained in the same terms. Following them was Pythagoras, who believed that numbers govern everything. This was (to our knowledge) the first statement of the possibility of a unified field theory: the concept of a mathematical equation that would explain and connect all aspects of reality.

Later, in the fourth century B.C., Plato argued that reality was made up of two very different kinds of things, needing two different kinds of explanation to deal with them. They were the perceptions of our senses (which are constantly changing) and the objects of thoughts ("ideas" or "forms," which are unchangeable). When Plato died in 347 B.C., he was replaced as the head of his philosophical school, the Academy in Athens, by a mathematician named Speusippus, who followed Pythagoras in believing in the existence of a mathematical theory that explained everything. (Tradition says that even in Plato's time, the Academy had a sign over the front entrance that said, "Let no one ignorant of geometry enter"). A young student named Aristotle disagreed. He left the Academy and, after a period of tutoring the young Alexander the Great, opened a competing school, the Lyceum, next door to Plato's.

This may seem like (and is) ancient history, but as this chapter will demonstrate, it has had a very damaging effect on the human sciences, particularly psychology and psychic research.

Medieval thought generally accepted that in order to describe reality, two very different kinds of approaches were needed: that of sensory observation, reason, and logic on the one hand; and that of faith and revelation on the other. The major problem of this time was how to reconcile the two and which kinds of questions could be answered by which approach. Thomas Aquinas (whose major project was to reconcile Aristotle's thought with Roman Catholic doctrine) believed that the first method—reason and sensory experience—could answer all questions except three. These three, which he believed could only be answered by faith and revelation, were:

1. how something could have appeared out of nothing
2. the triune nature of God
3. the part Jesus plays in the salvation of humankind

Out of the Renaissance, with its openness to new ideas combined with a continuing belief in one God who made everything, came the Enlightenment, that great revolution of human thought that led to modern science. The thought of the Enlightenment was based on five axioms:

1. There is a rational order of eternal truths. There is one and only one such order. All parts of this truth fit together and do not contradict each other. Everything works on the same principles. They always have and always will.
2. The human mind can understand both the parts and the whole of this truth—the trees and the forest.
3. The only way to truth is through objectifying reality and observing it rationally, without emotion, and with the tools of reason, logic, and mathematics.
4. Human beings can act in accordance with this pattern of truth. To do so will make our lives much better.
5. The universe is consistent in its operation, from the movements of the field mouse to those of the furthest galaxies. Since Newton showed that this rationality operated mechanically in the movements of the planets as well as in cogs and wheels on the earth, all the universe operates on mechanical

grounds. And machines have no free will. Every action is inexorable and determined.

Science grew up in the seventeenth and eighteenth centuries, a time when the primary worldview still held that the cosmos had been made by one God—a rational God. This was seen as a matter of common sense. The cosmos was therefore rational, and there was only one meaning to the term *rational*. The task of science was to understand this unified rational structure of the universe. In this view, which was then the standard view of Western culture, all things, having been made by one rational God, functioned in the same way. Even the Bible seemed to support this view. Genesis recounts how after the Flood, God put a "bow in the sky" as his sign that hereafter the universe would be run logically and consistently as "season would follow season." There would be no more whims or tantrums governing the shape of reality and what happened to it. Today, although mainstream science has discarded its belief in God, it still holds to the tenet that there is one rationality governing the entire cosmos. Whoever doubts it is seen a superstitious heretic.

Built into the growing field of science and our structure of knowledge, then, were the assumptions that the world is rational and that there is only one meaning to the term *rational*; that the world is consistent in its rationality; that all phenomena in it can be understood in the same way. There is one rationality, and everything from atoms to galaxies, from dreams to machines, from human behavior to the stroke of lightning in the sky, can be understood in its terms. Everything works in the same way. Deepening and widening this apparently unified understanding is the work of science.

Gradually in the history of science, this concept of the one rationality was clarified and made more precise, and some of the basic laws of the concept were formulated. The earliest scientific progress was made in that realm of experience in which things could be seen and touched. In this realm things could be added and subtracted, and so it seemed obvious from this one fact that *since part of the universe was quantitative, then everything in the universe was quantitative.* From this it was concluded that a field of science progresses only to the degree that it makes its data quantitative. This became a basic tenet of the scientific faith. So strong was this belief that people failed to realize that quantification (counting and measuring) is a human activity imposed on our knowledge of reality. Leibniz's famous statement "God is a mathematician" expressed this viewpoint clearly. A concept first formulated by Pythagoras over 2,500 years before was now accepted as natural law.

The logical next step is to contend that anything that can be counted and measured is quantifiable and has no free will. Two marbles and two marbles are four marbles. They cannot spontaneously decide to be five marbles.

Such an approach seemed to hold good in the new science of physics. The human sciences evolving in the late nineteenth century accepted these ideas. In light of the tremendous progress that physics had made by using them over the previous hundred years, it seemed obvious that physics had the correct method and axioms for science. Students of the human sciences therefore adopted concepts that fit the objects of study of nineteenth-century physics but were completely wrong for their own objects of study. This led to some pretty strange conclusions. The prevailing view that mechanism ruled the universe resulted in several very unfortunate muddles.

Freud. The mind is like a hydraulic pump, and everything in it can be explained mechanically. If an emotion was pressed out of consciousness, it could squirt out elsewhere as sublimation or reaction formation. This helped in understanding some pathology but left a great deal out. That it failed to explain things like genius, love, compassion, creativity, and dignity was noted, but this consideration did not change or affect Freud's basic ideas.

Marx. Society works like clockwork—inexorably, mechanically. History proceeded in a scientifically analyzable way through the dialectic of class struggle. This theory was supposed to predict the next century at least. It predicted nothing, including where communism would first develop (Marx did not believe it would reach Russia until it had triumphed in the West), the tragic and disastrous history of the Stalin era in the Soviet Union, the rise of fascism, and most of the other great social developments of that era.

Darwin. Although Darwin himself said practically nothing about evolution, his followers did. Species develop, succeed, or become extinct on mechanistic grounds. Random changes and mutations govern—and entirely explain—the appearance of new species. This theory must be stretched to its limits to account for such things as eggs (an enormous number of mutations have had to transpire at the same moment to produce a functional egg), and even with this intellectual stretching is very unconvincing. Science is reluctant to admit this fact, since it smacks of what has come to be known as "intelligent design," but we *must* move past the idea that our only choice is between two explanatory systems, God or Darwin. This is an extremely simplistic point of view. It is great for arguments, but very poor for increasing understanding.

Pavlov and Watson (and later Skinner). The damage done to a developing science of psychology by these underlying assumptions was major. If all the universe operates according to the same principles and what we could see or touch was quantitative and therefore determined, then the mind was also quantitative and determined. It could be reduced to the combinations of basic elements. How a person felt or acted was determined by conditioning. The present situation—the "state of the system"—absolutely determined what came next.

All these worldviews presuppose some kind of mechanistic basis to the universe. But since machines are incapable of goal-oriented behavior, teleology—the idea that "purpose" exists in the universe— became a dirty word in science and remains so to this day. By this view, if you think you are walking down the street to buy a newspaper, you are deluded. Both goal-oriented behavior and the free will to act according to the wish to attain a goal were regarded as delusions, although very powerful ones. Even as far back as the eighteenth century, this belief held such power that Samuel Johnson could say, "All theory is against free will. All experience is for it."

This kind of dogma led to a great deal of wasted effort in psychology and also to a great deal of silliness. In the mid–twentieth century, if I had stood up in a lecture hall and said, "All people are determined and have no free will," I would probably have been made head of my department. If, on the other hand, I said, "*I* am determined and have no free will; I am a robot who moves helplessly according to how I have been conditioned," I would very likely have been sent to a psychiatrist.

Or pity the poor psychoanalyst treating a patient with such an approach, who is also in analysis himself. As long as he is lying on the couch, everything he does or has done is determined, and free choice is not a relevant term. It is, at best, an illusion. After a session, he gets up and walks across the room to the therapist's chair. A patient comes in, and suddenly it is the *patient* who is determined and the analyst who has free will. He can now speak and act according to his best judgment.

Some years ago I went to a psychiatrist of that persuasion. His hobby was photography, and he had some beautiful photographs on the wall that he himself had taken. We parted after it became clear that he regarded his photography as springing from his creativity and done under free will. He also regarded my avocation of doing research as springing from my compulsions, which sprang from . . . (we won't go into that). Consequently, I had no free will. When it became clear that we could not come to an agreement on this point, we ended our relationship—amicably on my part.

It is largely as a result of its rigid dogma that the mind operates as a machine that orthodox psychoanalysis is now a matter of historical interest only. The historian Will Durant once remarked, "Psychoanalysis is not an art, it is not a science. It is the defense of a hero." And yet we can reflect that Freud, that profound, suffering, utterly courageous giant who, because of his well-demonstrated ability to grow and change would, if he were alive today, in all likelihood be anti-Freudian!

Another part of the Enlightenment view developed following René Descartes' belief that a science was real and could make progress only if you could quantify the data. A nonquantitative science was fit only as a hobby for rich people. Descartes even contended that there was no point in studying history because you cannot quantify the data. Even if you studied the history of Rome all your life, you still would not know about it as much as did "Cicero's servant girl."

Taking this view to heart, a major school of psychology—the behaviorists—realizing that consciousness could not be quantified, came up with a solution so weird that it has been remarked, "Behaviorism does not need a rebuttal. It needs a cure." The behaviorists solution was that they would pretend, in talking to each other, and in acting as professional psychologists, that consciousness did not exist. Running away from its primary (or any other) datum is a poor way to try to do science. It would be like the astronomers pretending that stars did not exist because such phenomena did not fit their theories.

The disaster that is psychology is well known. After over a hundred years of work by many thousands of dedicated men and women, publishing more books and journals than one cares to think about, very little has been learned. Some rules of thumb, some unconnected theories accepted by some and not by others, some techniques, are about all we have to show. We have not been able to study the things that make us specifically human—compassion, love, dignity, courage—the things that Plato said "keep us on two legs instead of four." There is more about being human in a volume of Tolstoy or Dostoyevsky or the plays of Shakespeare than there is in the psychology textbooks used in our colleges.

A great deal of this situation is due to the belief in a mathematical unified field theory, the belief that all the cosmos works in the same way and can be studied in the same way and that physics was so successful that we should use its concepts and methods even though the material we study is very different. For example, "The body is by nature divisible. The mind is by nature indivisible," said Descartes. You cannot study a divisible field in the same way you study an indivisible one, a "seamless garment." If you try, you will have no more success than the physicists who try to develop a single mathematics that includes the "lumpy" universe of the very small (in quantum physics, nature makes leaps; things come in packets that interact with each other) with the "smooth," flowing relativity universe of the very large. (According to the old adage, *Natura non facit saltus*—"Nature makes no leaps.")

An even worse situation exists in the field of psychical research. The field came into existence in the mid- to late-nineteenth century, when the popularity of spiritualism led scientists to begin to investigate these strange phenomena. After the first half century or so, psychical research had yielded two separate kinds of data.

First, there were the large, meaningful events that had excited so much interest: deathbed apparitions, instances of precognition, poltergeist activity, and so forth. These did not just occur at random. They had some meaning, even if we did not know exactly what it was. They let the observer know that something important and out of the ordinary had happened, something that had real meaning, even if we could not discover at the moment what that meaning was. The psychiatrist Jan Ehrenwald has called these events "need-determined."

The Carrington episode presented at the beginning of this book illustrates this kind of case. It is plain that there was both a need and a paranormal event. At this time we do not know how to proceed further. We do not know how to explain it, how to most fruitfully construe the data. Shall we call it "telepathy" and let it go at that? In that case, all we are doing is giving a name to the fact that Mrs. Garrett had information she could not have acquired by the route of the ordinary senses. Shall we try to ascertain who or what was the primary agent in this action and who or what the secondary? Or are these terms even applicable? Shall we call it "spirit intervention," if we can accept the metaphysical implications of this term? And, if we can, why did it occur in this case and not in others where the need was as great or greater? We know that something both important and paranormal was going on, but not what it was.

One of our best parapsychological researchers, Gertrude Schmeidler, once said that the study of psychic phenomena—*psi* for short—is like walking around a patch of dense forest. Something big is in the forest. We can see trees shaking and hear noises. But we cannot see what the animal is or what it is like. We only know that it is there, and that it is big.

The second kind of psychic phenomena are the data produced in the laboratory by such actions as clairvoyant or telepathic card guessing, where the sum total of the guesses is statistically above reasonable chance levels. The subject does not know if he or she has, with a specific card, made a correct or incorrect guess. If the subject is told that a particular guess is correct, it will have no special meaning. (Ehrenwald has called this type of psi "flaw-determined." He theorizes that it seems to result from a small random failure in whatever system keeps us from having more psi events.)

This second, "flaw-determined" type of psi can be quantified. If the results are above chance, this can be demonstrated precisely and statistically. Such events can be produced in a laboratory, like most of the data of physics. Once psychic researchers had achieved such results, they felt that they could make their field "scientific" and have it accepted by the rest of science.

Before we proceed, let me digress to provide a word about terminology. Over the years, those working in the field of paranormal events have developed a convention. The type of occurrence that can be studied in the laboratory—the "flaw-determined" event that we see in card and random-number guessing—is called *parapsychology*. The study of the larger, more spontaneous, "need-determined" type, such as deathbed apparitions and telepathy in emergencies (for example, the Hinchliffe incident), has been called *psychical research*. The two terms are not rigidly defined and to some degree are used interchangeably; however, the distinction tends to remain. This book is primarily concerned with the "need-determined" type of event, so I shall be generally using the term *psychical research*.

Unlike "flaw-determined" types of phenomena, which can be and have been studied quantitatively, the "need-determined" type cannot be produced on demand in a laboratory; it cannot be quantified. Researchers believed that you could not have a science if things are unpredictable and "hop about," and these large-scale meaningful events certainly seem to hop about. For this reason, many of the scientists in the field abandoned the study of need-determined events and concentrated on studying the other type in various laboratories.

In so doing, they were following an exhortation by one of the founders of modern parapsychological research, the nineteenth-century British philosopher Henry Sidgwick: "If they will not believe fifty experiments, give them fifty more and then another fifty until they must believe." We have certainly done this with far more experiments than Sidgwick suggested. For reasons I will discuss later, the data of psychical research have still not been accepted by the scientific mainstream—not necessarily for scientific reasons. I am reminded of the noted mathematician Warren Weaver. After attesting to the soundness of the experiments of J. B. Rhine, the pioneering parapsychologist at Duke University, as well as to Rhine's personal integrity, Weaver wrote, "I end by concluding that I cannot explain away Professor Rhine's evidence and I cannot accept it."

The abandonment of need-determined paranormal events in favor of the flaw-determined types accomplished two things. It made the researchers feel more scientific, even though it did not win them acceptance in the scientific community. It also succeeded in the almost impossible task of making psychical research dull and boring.

Ernest Jones, one of Freud's closest disciples, reports how shocked he was to learn that Freud believed in telepathy. He said to Freud, "If we are prepared to consider the possibility of mental processes floating in the air, what is to stop us from believing in angels?" Freud replied, "Quite so. And even *der liebe Gott.*" A science of psychical and parapsychological research may or may not lead us in the direction of a "beloved God," but we must be prepared for it to lead us to some startling places.

The general view of the world we live in—in the most profound sense, our home—is the bedrock on which we rest and on whose solidity our personality stands. It is so much a part of us that we can hardly see it. (There is an old joke about who first discovered water. The answer, of course, is that we don't know who it was, but we do know that it was not a fish!)

If this world-picture, our view of how things are and work, is threatened, we feel a strong, although undifferentiated, anxiety. This is what the German psychiatrist Kurt Goldstein called "catastrophic anxiety," the unverbalized sense that if this discordance is not removed, our whole personality organization is at risk. There is an unconscious pressure to somehow get rid of the disruptive material. Sometimes this is done by forgetting it or by draining the emotion out of it and remembering it in a curious sort of black-and-white manner with no solid meaning. We can decide that these things are, to quote the philosopher Jacob Needleman, "bubbles of mystery floating around in an otherwise normal universe."[2] The only function of these "bubbles" is to give us good stories to tell at a dinner party without ever questioning their meanings or implications. If they are presented as scientific data, we can deal with them intellectually as if they had no implications for us or for other human beings. We can comfortably decide that there must be something wrong with the experiment or observation and that if we took the trouble to search for the error, we could find it. Or we can declare, as Henry Sidgwick back in the 1880s predicted we would, that "the experimenter is in on the trick." By and large, the scientific community has reacted to the data of psychical research in a manner similar to the famous farmer who, on seeing a giraffe for the first time, stated, "There ain't no such animal."

Today we have another method of distancing ourselves from the implications of what we are observing. We can decide that, since the science of quantum mechanics is so full of mysterious concepts, the "explanation" of psi must lie there. Thus there is really no problem; everything about psi has already been explained by quantum science, or will be very soon. Forty years ago, I was one of the people who started the idea that psi could be explained in terms of quantum mechanics or relativity theory. I now believe that we were wrong, and I regret my part in it. Dignity, love, loyalty, awe, and psi must be dealt with on their own terms in a science built on these observables, not one built on the observables of subatomic particles.

The paranormal makes us feel terribly threatened, but if our age has shown us anything, it is our great flexibility and our ability to absorb new ideas, to incorporate extensions of our basic, sense-derived, Newtonian view of reality, and to do this without collapsing or suffering anything more than irritation. In their different ways Freud, Einstein, and Picasso showed that we can enlarge our world picture without shattering like glass under a hammer. We see something like this going on today as the world slowly and awkwardly accepts the new idea of the importance of ecology and the need to stop fouling our own nest. It took us a while with each of these new extensions, but now they are a part of our culture and our bedrock view of reality. So it will be with psi.

One point is central to the whole problem of psi. If the whole cosmos—everything, that is—works on the same principles and laws, psi is impossible and therefore does not happen. The laws, the basic limiting principles, of our daily life work far too well to be invalid. They are true, and under them psi events cannot occur. Therefore all paranormal events are due to bad observation, coincidence, poor memory, or outright lying. Since we are so deeply committed to the concept of the consistency of reality—of everything, everywhere working on the same principles—this seems to settle the matter. Psi events do not happen, or, if they do, they are some sort of exception and are ultimately unimportant.

Nevertheless, we have learned in the past hundred years or so that different laws, different basic limiting principles, apply to different segments of reality. Cause and effect rule in the segment revealed by our senses but not in the microcosm, the realm of the very small. Our senses reveal a world with discrete observables; our inner life, our consciousness, does not. Statements made about the macrocosm, the spaces between the stars, are meaningless when applied to the spaces between buildings or cities. What is "normal" in one realm of experience is paranormal in another. What can be said or done in one realm cannot be said or done in another. You cannot make statements about the color, shape, or temperature of a subatomic particle, although you can make such a statement about an object in the realm of the senses. You can talk about a table that is standing still, but not about an electron that is not in motion. You can legitimately use words such as *morality, ethics,* or *purpose* in certain segments, such as those of human consciousness or interactions, but not in segments concerning the falling of a stone or the growth of a flower.

Since we began to understand scientific inquiry in the seventeenth century, we have also learned a hard lesson that we often forget: When the fact and the theory collide head–on, we limit or abandon the theory. We do this even if the theory is a cherished one about how things are and work. We do *not* deny the fact or the importance of its existence. The classic example of this is Alexander Fleming's discovery of penicillin. Among many petri dishes with bacteria, he responded to one in which the bacteria did *not* grow or flourish. He did *not* decide that this particular sample was nonexistent, unimportant, or an exception. He allowed himself to be surprised.

The existence of psi events demonstrates that there is a segment of perceived reality, a realm of experience, in which such events are valid and "normal." We will have to work toward an understanding of that segment and its laws and basic limiting principles. One way to move forward in this direction is to remember St. Augustine's statement, "There are no such things as miracles which violate the laws of nature. There are only events which violate our limited knowledge of the laws of nature." As we learn more about the laws of nature that apply to psi (and we must do this by developing a science of psi on its own terms), we will find that the laws extend our view of reality instead of—as we often fear—destroying it. Our sensorially derived view of "what is," by means of which we survive biologically, will still be absolutely valid. But, as Freud, Einstein, Planck, and Picasso showed when they expanded our view of reality, there will be more. And the "more" will open new vistas, new possibilities, new ways of comprehending what we human beings are and what we may become. As the great French philosopher Henri Bergson said in his 1913 presidential address to the Society for Psychical Research (SPR),

"Nature has far more secrets to reveal than have yet been disclosed. . . . The last thing that the scientist will say—if he is a true one—is, 'The thing is impossible.'"

After the last century of scientific advancement, very few scientists would doubt that Bergson's statement is still as true as it has always been.

Psi is a terribly important adventure. It is the wild card in our seemingly hopeless attempt to get the human race off the endangered-species list. As the physicist and psychic researcher Robert McConnell showed at the hundredth-anniversary meeting of the Society for Psychical Research in 1982, we treat something according to how we perceive and define it. I may regard this piece of furniture as a table (to put things on), as firewood (to burn), as a couch (to lie down on), as junk (to throw out), or as art (to take to a museum). Unless we can change the way we regard and define human beings, we will not be able to stop killing each other and poisoning our only planet. Psychic research has the data to give us a new way to view ourselves and each other.

Both need-determined and flaw-determined events have tremendous implications for the nature of human beings and the structure of the universe. The difference is that with the flaw-determined events—the small, card-guessing type of events—you can concentrate on your statistics and pretty much ignore the implications. (Or you can amuse and distract yourself by trying to "explain" them with concepts from quantum physics.) You cannot remain comfortable with the large, need-determined events such as the two described at the beginning of this chapter.

But we must have courage. We must be open to facing the possibility that we will find things so new and startling that they change our preconceptions about ourselves and about the universe we live in. So far, we have not had that courage. Perhaps now with species extinction looming before us, we will find that courage. The possibility of a great adventure is before us.[3]

Case History

"The Lost Harp"
Elizabeth L. Mayer

My eleven-year-old daughter, Meg, who'd fallen in love with the harp at age six, had begun performing. She wasn't playing a classical pedal harp but a smaller, extremely valuable instrument built and carved by a master harp-maker. After a Christmas concert, her harp was stolen from the theater where she was playing. For two months we went through every conceivable channel trying to locate it: the police, instrument dealers across the country, the American Harp Society newsletters—even a CBS-TV news story. Nothing worked.

Finally, a wise and devoted friend told me, "If you really want that harp back, you should be willing to try anything. Try calling a dowser." The only thing I knew about dowsers were that they were that strange breed who locate underground water with forked sticks. But according to my friend, the "really good" dowsers can locate not just water but lost objects as well.

Finding lost objects with *forked sticks?* Well, nothing was happening on the police front, and my daughter, spoiled by several years of playing an extraordinary instrument, had found the series of commercial harps we'd rented simply unplayable. So, half-embarrassed but desperate, I decided to take my friend's dare. I asked her if she could locate a really good dowser—the best, I said. She promptly called the American Society of Dowsers and came back with the phone number of the society's current president, Harold McCoy, in Fayetteville, Arkansas.*

---

*Shortly after finding my harp, Harold McCoy founded the Ozark Research Institute, whose mission is to conduct research into such phenomena as hands-on and remote healing, map dowsing, thought forms, and other fields of "thought power." ORI (www.ozarkresearch.org) currently has three thousand members in twenty-four countries.

Reprinted from Elizabeth L. Mayer, *Extraordinary Knowing: Science, Skepticism, and the Inexplicable Powers of the Human Mind* (New York: Bantam Dell, 2007), 2–4.

I called him that day. Harold picked up the phone—friendly, cheerful, heavy Arkansas accent. I told him I'd heard he could dowse for lost objects and that I'd had a valuable harp stolen in Oakland, California. Could he help me locate it?

"Give me a second," he said. "I'll tell you if it's still in Oakland." He paused, then: "Well, it's still there. Send me a street map of Oakland, and I'll locate the harp for you." Skeptical—but what, after all, did I have to lose?—I promptly overnighted him a map. Two days later, he called back. "Well, I got that harp located," he said. "It's in the second house on the right on D—— Street, just off L—— Avenue."

I'd never heard of either street. But I did like the sound of the man's voice—whoever he was. And I don't like backing down on a dare. Why not drive to the house he'd identified? At least I'd get the address. I looked on an Oakland map and found the neighborhood. It was miles from anywhere I'd ever been. I got in my car, drove into Oakland, located the house, wrote down the number, called the police, and told them I'd gotten a tip that the harp might be at that house. Not good enough for a search warrant, they said. They were going to close the case—there was no way this unique, portable, and highly marketable item hadn't already been sold; it was gone forever.

But I found I couldn't quite let it go. Was it the dare? Was it my admiration for the friend who'd instigated the whole thing? Was it my devastated daughter? Or was it just that I had genuinely liked the sound of that voice on the other end of the line?

I decided to post flyers in a two-block area around the house, offering a reward for the harp's return. It was a crazy idea, but why not? I put up flyers in those two blocks, and only those two blocks. I was embarrassed enough about what I was doing to tell just a couple of close friends about it.

Three days later, my phone rang. A man's voice told me he'd seen a flyer outside his house describing a stolen harp. He said it was exactly the harp his next-door neighbor had recently obtained and showed him. He wouldn't give me his name or number, but offered to get the harp returned to me. And two weeks later, after a series of circuitous telephone calls, he told me to meet a teenage boy at 10:00 p.m., in the rear parking lot of an all-night Safeway. I arrived to find a young man loitering in the lot. He looked at me and said, "The harp?" I nodded. Within minutes, the harp was in the back of my station wagon, and I drove off.

Twenty-five minutes later, as I turned into my driveway, I had the thought: *This changes everything.*

I was right. The harp changes how I work as a clinician and psychoanalyst. It changed the nature of the research I pursued. It changed my sense of what's ordinary and what's extraordinary. Most of all, it changed my relatively established, relatively contented, relatively secure sense of how the world adds up. If Harold McCoy did what he appeared to have done, I had to face the fact that my notions of space, time, reality, and the nature of the human mind were stunningly inadequate. Disturbing as that recognition was, there was something intriguing, even exciting, about it as well.

Over the ensuing months, I spent a lot of sleepless nights. I argued with myself a lot. I regularly woke up at 3:00 a.m., certain that with just a little more effort, a little more clear thinking, I'd come up with some comfortably rational way to explain how that harp had ended up back in my living room where it belonged. Finally a friend of mine, a statistics professor at Berkeley, listened to my conflicted ranting and said in exasperation: "Get *over* it and get some sleep, Lisby. As a statistician, I can promise you the odds that dowsing works are a lot greater than the odds that this could have been coincidence."

2

What Do We Now Know about Psychic Phenomena?

The actual cannot be impossible.
—Gustav Theodor Fechner

Before we begin our attempt to design a science of meaningful psychic events, let us review what we now know. What has come out of the last hundred-years-plus in which a great many men and women, often of the highest caliber, have studied this field? Not knowing where we are before we set out reminds me of the psychologist Abraham Maslow's story of the airplane pilot who radioed back to base, "We're lost, but we're making wonderful time!"

This is not the place to review the voluminous literature of this work. This has been well done elsewhere, and references at the back of this book will lead anyone there who wants to go. What I will do is summarize what we know to be true from this extensive exploration and what we believe extremely likely to be true. We *do* know much more than we think we know. Let us take a hypothetical situation.

There are two pairs of individuals. The first, Joe and Jim, are both corporate lawyers, both are six feet tall, both have one brown eye and one gray eye, and both have a dog named Spot. One lives in New York, the other eight hundred miles away in Chicago. They have never heard of each other and have never crossed paths. The second pair is Harry and Lucy. He is an artist, she is a scientist. He likes the opera, she prefers baseball games. He is five feet, eleven inches tall; she is five feet two. He lives in Baltimore; she lives nearly three thousand miles away in Los Angeles. Ten years ago they had a brief, intense affair and have not spoken to or heard anything of each other since that time.

In each pair, one of them dies unexpectedly in an automobile accident. In one pair, the survivor sees a deathbed apparition of the other. The one who dies suddenly appears to the other, in a form so real that the living one believes he (or she) is actually seeing the person, then makes some sort of eye or other contact and disappears just as suddenly. The number of such well-attested cases is so large that we have pretty much stopped publishing them in the psychical research journals.

In which pair does the deathbed apparition appear—Joe and Jim, or Harry and Lucy?

For anyone with any experience in this field, and for most of the rest of us, there is no question. It is clearly Harry and Lucy.

We do understand certain aspects of the paranormal. Research over the past hundred-plus years has led us some distance. The following facts have emerged and now can be considered definitely proven.

1. Sometimes people unequivocally demonstrate having specific, concrete information that could not have been attained through sensory channels or from extrapolation of data achieved through the senses. If this information was known to any other individual at that time, we conventionally label this phenomenon "telepathy." If the information was not known to anyone else but existed in some testable form, we call the phenomenon "clairvoyance." If the information does not yet exist in clock-calendar time, we call the phenomenon "precognition."

2. Space or other physical factors (such as walls or the curvature of the earth) between the source of the original informa-

tion and the person who demonstrates having it is not a factor. Telepathy seems to operate in about the same manner whether it comes from a thousand miles away or from only as far as the next room.

3. Emotional factors are the major (and indeed only) factors we know of linking the apparent origin of the information and the person who demonstrates having the knowledge. But there are almost certainly other kinds of links that we do not now know about.

4. Many people become anxious when they hear or read of examples of psi, or encounter affirmations of the existence of psi.

The strength of this anxiety should not be underestimated. It has led to the wholesale rejection of the data of parapsychological research by a large number of people in terms far more extreme than they would use in other areas. Consider, for example, the early nineteenth-century natural philosopher Alexander von Humboldt, one of the greatest scientists of recent centuries. He stated that no matter what the evidence for the existence of psi was, he would not believe it: "Neither the testimony of all the Fellows of the Royal Society, nor even the evidence of my own senses, could lead me to believe in the transmission of thought from one person to another independently of the recognised channels of sensation. It is clearly impossible." He chose to give up his lifelong attitudes toward science and the scientific method rather than consider changing them. Here is a great scientist stating that he knows so much about reality that the universe holds no more surprises for him. No doubt this is a comforting and reassuring belief, but it is an astonishing one for a scientist to hold.[1]

In any event, this is all we know for certain about large, meaningful psychic events. At this point we must be very careful about the ways we formulate this knowledge. Terms such as *sender, receiver, energy, transmission,* and many others carry a heavy baggage of implications. These can unconsciously influence our thinking and our attempts to solve problems.

So much for what we *know* in psychical and parapsychological research. After more than a century of study, the verdict is in on these facts. Whoever questions them simply has not done his or her homework.

However, other particulars in this field are less certain. These are particulars that anyone familiar with the field regards as *almost* certainly true, but about which a small doubt remains. These particulars include:

1. Neither of the two most widely talked-about hypotheses to explain the data is adequate. The first hypothesis, referred to as "super-ESP," is that all the evidence can be explained by some form of telepathy or clairvoyance. The second hypothesis is that the evidence can be explained by the existence of discarnate entities. That these two, or either of them, might or might not be valid is not the point here. Neither of these two precludes the other. Each seems to be a reasonable explanation for *some* of the events, but together or separately they are far from satisfactory as a way to formulate or explain all the events of which we have solid evidence. A third explanatory system is needed, which might conceivably include either or both of the first two.

2. Relative physical motion between the source of the information and the person who acquired it is not a factor.

3. Large-scale psi events are related to the constellation of emotions surrounding the person or thing involved.

4. The laws sometimes said to apply to magic (in the sense used, for example, by J. G. Frazer in his classic study *The Golden Bough*) do not apply to the psychic. These primary laws of magic are:
   The law of similarity. If two things resemble each other in one way, they resemble and affect each other in other ways also. If a plant has heart-shaped leaves, it can affect the heart. If I sprinkle water on the ground in the proper ceremony, it is likely to bring rain.

  The law of contiguity. If two things were once connected, they are always connected. If, for instance, I put your discarded fingernails on a doll and stab the doll, you will feel the pain.

These two laws do not govern the formation of large-scale psychic events.

5. The time barrier can sometimes be breached. In both large-scale events and small-scale studies, people have sometimes shown knowledge of events that could not have been extrapolated from presently existing data and that had not yet occurred in clock-calendar time.

6. If a person has information that he or she very much desires to keep secret, it cannot be attained psychically by other persons.

7. If a person attains psychic information and knows that it came from another person, the recipient cannot tell whether it was on the surface of the other person's mind or was far from her present awareness.

8. Under rare conditions, the specifics of which are unknown, psychological intent can affect the movement of matter.[2]

9. There is something in or relating to the human personality that does not cease to exist at the moment of bodily death. (A large percentage of deathbed apparitions occur a measurable interval after the death of the body.)

A fascinating suggestion was made by two of our most knowledgeable and careful workers in the field of psi, Justa Smith and Charles Honorton. Although new (at least to me) and not accepted in the field to the degree the other concepts listed here are, it has such potential that it seems worth adding to the list. At the very least, I believe it would make most students of psi deeply thoughtful.

Justa Smith, a biochemist, had been working with a very well-reputed psychic healer named Oskar Estebany and some other healers. They were trying to influence enzymes in test tubes. To her surprise, if the enzymes had been in a human body, the effect in each case would have been to improve the person's health. Smith commented, in part:

> We used three different enzymes with all the healers. Each had their own samples. We used trypsin, NADH, and glucophosphotase. The trypsin was increased in effect which would be a helpful thing. The phosphotase decreased its activity which would be helpful in a positive direction. The NADH was not affected, but NADH is in balance so any change would have been unhelpful. My conclusion is that the effect on enzymes by a healer is always in a positive, helpful direction. The healers did not know which enzymes were being used or in which direction change would be helpful. None of them had any training in enzymology.

Honorton observed:

> That sounds extremely important. When we are working on PK [psychokinesis, or mentally influencing physical objects] with a random generator in the next room, the effect on the generated series of numbers is in the direction of greater order. When the participant shows evidence of PK, the random numbers become less random and more orderly. It does not matter what the source of the randomness is, thermal noise, radioactive delay, etc., the ordering is in a positive direction. It seems to be goal-directed.[3]

Everything we know, including all the data from psychic healing, seems to indicate that psi effects have a positive, goal-directed orientation. Furthermore, this direction goes beyond the learned knowledge of the participants. Knowledge of medicine, for example, does not help people get better results with psychic healing.

If you are a participant in any developing field of human knowledge and you survey your colleagues, you will find that they fall into three classes. On your left are those who believe more than you do (the wild-haired, soft-headed group). On your right are those who believe less than you do (the rigid, uptight conservatives). Immediately in front of you is a small group of colleagues who agree with you on what to believe and disbelieve. (These are the intelligent, knowledge-able people!)

This is certainly true in the field of psychic research. Nonetheless, I strongly believe that the centrist approach of this chapter is in agreement with the overwhelming majority of those who have studied this area. Some may wish to move one or more of the statements from the "probably true" list to the "already proven" list. But I do not think that anyone seriously conversant with the field would move any of the statements in the opposite direction or take them off both lists.

This, then, is the present state of affairs in our knowledge of psi. We *do* know a good deal. It is a solid base from which to set out on the next phase of our foray. In chapter 4, I will show how a real science of large-scale, meaningful psi events can be designed.

Case History

A Call to the Wimbledon Underground
Lawrence LeShan

Rosalind Heywood was a lovely upper-class English lady. She had been in the Nursing Corps in Gallipoli in World War I. Her husband had been a colonel in one of the British Indian regiments and now worked in central London, to which he commuted every day by car, returning home about six or seven o'clock. He was a slim, vigorous man who was believed to be in excellent health. At the time of this incident (the mid-1970s), the family lived in Wimbledon, a suburb of London, on the last stop of one of the Underground lines.

Over the years, Mrs. Heywood occasionally had unusual psychic experiences. She would become aware that she had to *do* something, often of a seemingly meaningless nature. She called these experiences "orders." After she had carried them out, she would find that they had been important and of a positive nature. (In a way, this was the opposite of Socrates's *daimon*, his inner voice, which only told him *not* to do something he was considering. Her "orders" told her only to do something.)

One apparently ordinary day, she was at home when she unexpectedly "received orders." She was to go to the local train station (about a mile from her home) and meet the three o'clock train. Since her car was with her husband in London, she went to a neighbor's house to borrow her car. The neighbor told me, approximately three weeks later, that Mrs. Heywood had seemed calm but communicated a sense of urgency. She had simply said she needed the neighbor's car immediately with no further details.

In town, at about this time, her husband had suffered a heart attack. Nothing like this had ever happened to him before. Confused and disoriented, he could think of nothing to do except go home. He took the train to Wimbledon station, arrived there at three o'clock, weakly climbed the stairs to the street, and was wondering how to get home.

30

Mrs. Heywood saw him, put him in the car, and immediately drove to the local hospital. He was quickly put in intensive care. Later her physician told her (and still later confirmed to me) that if he had been an hour later, they probably could not have saved him. As it was, he recovered well.

3

Normal and
Paranormal Communication

*It is curious to reflect that the things humans understand best
are, on the whole, the things that least concern them. They
can predict the movements of the planets, but not the weath-
er; they have fathomed the deep sea, but cannot measure
their own desires; they know more about beer than about
their blood . . . and the heart of all their knowledge is a
mystery: how they acquire it.*
— Paraphrased from C. W. E. Mundle,
"Strange Facts in Search of a Theory"

Before we proceed, there is one thing more about psi that we
believe to be almost certainly true. It concerns the great similarities
between "normal" and "paranormal" communication. Because this
point is complex and needs more clarification than the others I have
made, I have devoted a separate chapter to it.

We shall begin by clarifying the term *paranormal*. How does a
"paranormal occurrence" differ from a "normal occurrence"? In other
words, what are the differences between situations in which information is received through the senses and those in which it is not?

So as not to prejudice our investigation in advance, let us rename
these two types of perception in neutral terms. Instead of the term

normal perception, let us use the term *type A perception.* And for *paranor-mal perception,* let us substitute *type B perception.* Without the emotional luggage of the concepts of "normal" and "paranormal," we may be able to see more clearly.

With the examples of the kind of psi occurrence that first focused our attention on type B perceptions, we come to the question of how they differ from "normal," type A perceptions. What distinguishes these two kinds of events from each other?

Certainly they *are* different. We feel this strongly. But wherein does the difference lie?

Let us start this exploration by asking a simple question. What is the difference between conditions favoring the occurrence of iden-tifiable type A and of identifiable type B perceptions? We have been studying normal, type A perceptions in the psychology laboratory for a hundred years now. What conclusions have been reached in these studies that are different from the conclusions reached in the study of paranormal, type B perceptions?

To our surprise, we find there are no differences. Conditions favoring the occurrence of type A perceptions also favor the occur-rence of type B. We might begin with the conclusions of Gardner Murphy, who spent a lifetime of study in both fields and who was president both of the American Psychological Association and of the American Society for Psychical Research:

> We make contact through the sensory processes and through the extrasensory processes in essentially the same way. . . . As far as psy-chology is concerned, the basic dynamics are the same in the two areas. Anything which helps us, for example, to perceive clearly at the level of normal perception helps us to perceive clearly at the level of extrasensory perception.

Murphy goes on to say:

> The same general laws which hold in all psychology, laws relating to the structuring of the world of perception, relating to the influ-ence of motivation upon such structuring, relating to the Gestalt

principles of membership, character, closure, salience, relating to the satiation of motives and the role of substitutes during such satiation . . . may be found to apply perfectly to paranormal perception.[1]

Elsewhere he wrote:

My own point of view would be simply that [in psychology and in parapsychology] we are dealing with the same classes of phenomena all the way through; that the motive power is the same in both fields; that whatever we learn from one type of investigation offers hypotheses which have a very large likelihood of being fulfilled when tried out in the other sphere.[2]

Similarly, summing up his long and rich studies, another psi researcher, René Warcollier, wrote, "In our investigations we have observed that the laws of normal and abnormal psychology apply to telepathy."[3] John Beloff, one of our most experienced and searching parapsychologists, makes the same point: "What happens . . . in ESP or PK . . . is essentially of the same nature as that which happens in our normal cognitive processes or in our normal voluntary behavior."[4] And J. B. Rhine, one of the most important figures in modern parapsychology, wrote:

[Psi] has already been found to show some of the familiar characteristics of such cognitive abilities as memory and learning. It responds positively to motivation and conditions favoring concentration of effort. Favorable attitudes toward psi capacity, toward the experimenter and toward the test situation appear rather uniformly to improve the operation of psi. The position of a given trial in the test structure reflects much the same configurational principles and pattern effects found in similar cognitive behavior. For example, tests involving a column of targets are likely to show greater success at the beginning and end of the column. . . . On the whole, the relationship of ESP scores to attitudes, school grades, intelligence quotients, extroversion, and the like show sufficient consistency to give assurance that a natural function of the personality is involved.[5]

It would be easy to multiply such quotations and to review the long years of careful laboratory experimentation that led to them. It does not seem necessary, however, to do this here. The facts are clear. Psychological and social conditions favoring "normal" perception also favor "paranormal" perception. Psychological and social conditions operating against normal perception also operate against paranormal perception. What then are the differences between them? To our surprise, we shall be able to find only two: (1) the location of the mystery; (2) the frequency of observed phenomena. Let us take these one at a time.

In each type of information, there is a mystery: a tremendous gap in our knowledge of how we acquired the information. In type A (normal perception), the gap concerns how the changes in our brain brought about by sensory stimulation were changed into conscious experience. We have brain changes. We then have conscious experience. These two resemble each other about as much—in Arthur S. Eddington's phrase—as a telephone number resembles a subscriber. How is one translated into the other? We do not know. The gap remains, for the time being, unbridgeable. As Eddington noted:

> Some influence . . . plays on the extremity of a nerve, starting a series of physical and chemical changes which are propagated along the nerve of a brain-cell; there a mystery happens, and an image or sensation arises in the mind which cannot purport to resemble the stimulus which excited it.[6]

In type B (paranormal) perception, the gap is practically as large. How does the information get from the original source to consciousness? I suddenly know that my daughter, five hundred miles away, has had a car accident. I even correctly know some of the details. How did the knowledge cross the "gap"? We do not know. The gap remains, for the time being, unbridgeable.

To use an analogy, it is as if there were a sealed room with no openings in the walls, floor, or ceiling. Through the walls (the senses), visitors (sensory perceptions) constantly "arrive." Occasionally a visitor (a paranormal perception) comes in through the ceiling. We have no idea how visitors can arrive through either route. We are, however, so used to their arriving through the walls that we cease to consider it mysterious. By contrast, the rare visitor through the ceiling arouses in us emotions of amazement. Then, when we begin to think about it, we feel that since there are no openings in the ceiling, such visits are "paranormal" and impossible. We forget that the same conclusions apply to our everyday, through-the-wall visitors.

The answer of the parapsychologist to the psychologist who demands to know how the paranormally acquired information could possibly have arrived in consciousness must be to apply the same question to the material the psychologist accepts without question in his or her daily work. Both are equally mysterious. As far as solutions to the problems go, the parapsychologist can legitimately say, "You show me yours, and I'll show you mine." As author Stuart Holroyd has observed, "The word *paranormal*, in fact, is not descriptive of events or faculties, but rather of the boundaries that give the Western cultural construct its shape."[7]

During the Second World War, a recruit was on guard duty on the outskirts of a training camp on the dusty Kansas plains. A sergeant (like sergeants from time immemorial) was making his life miserable by asking him all sorts of questions about his duty and orders. Finally the sergeant asked, "What would you do if you saw an enemy battleship coming across the plains toward the camp?" The recruit answered, "I'd call 'Up periscope' and torpedo it." The sergeant asked, "Where would you get your submarine?" The reply was, "The same place you got your damn battleship!" Parapsychologists can legitimately demand that psychologists solve their own "gap" problem with type A perceptions before categorically stating that the parapsychologists' "gap" makes type B perceptions impossible and invalid.

The biologist E. W. Sinnott wrote, "How such incompatible things as mind and body can be so closely knit together has been philosophy's perennial despair."[8] In 1910, the psychologist E. M. Weyer spoke of "that bridge of cobwebs, closed to science, spanning the chasm between conscious mind and insensate matter."[9] If one looks at the matter objectively, the mystery of how information "jumps" from Joe's central nervous system to his consciousness is just as great as the mystery of how the information "jumps" from Jane's consciousness to Joe's consciousness. In neither case do we know how to deal with the problem. C. E. M. Joad put the situation thus:

> We have not the faintest idea how the transition from event in the brain to experience in consciousness is effected. Hence the fact that there is an unbridgeable gulf in our knowledge of the mode by which what is going on in our mind is communicated to another is not so odd as it might first appear. There is an equally unbridgeable gap in our knowledge of the mode by which what is going on in the body and brain is communicated to the mind that animates them. We forget the mystery of the latter only because it is common; we are astonished by the oddness of the former only because it is rare.[10]

Thus the first real difference we find between type A and type B perceptions is in the location of the gap in our knowledge. In type A it is between our brain and our consciousness. In type B it is between someone else's consciousness (or the "target" object) and our consciousness. The mystery in each is just as great. We are, as Joad pointed out, astonished at one and not at the other because identified type A perceptions are common and everyday, and identifiable type B perceptions are not. The second difference we are able to find is thus in frequency of identifiable occurrence.[11]

Case History

"An Experience in the Forest"
Eda LeShan

Comment by Lawrence LeShan: The story below concerns an incident that happened to my wife, Eda LeShan, during the years when I was training people in psychic healing. I later interviewed the aunt involved, and she corroborated the story completely. The report that follows is in Eda's own words, as it appeared in her book *Eda LeShan: On Living Your Life*:

I found the first years of Larry's research intellectually stimulating, and finally I decided I wanted to have the direct emotional experience of being a member of one of his workshops in California. Paranormal experiences can be facilitated by training in the art of meditation, and learning how to meditate is very tough work. This was a five-day programme, in which we worked eight to ten hours a day, trying to gain control over our minds. There is nothing that is more difficult than doing just one thing at a time, and that is what meditation is really all about. It is training the mind in the same way that one can train the body for better physical control through exercise or weight lifting, or playing tennis.

I didn't really expect anything to happen to me; I was too practical, too down-to-earth; too set in the everyday reality of my senses to be able to have any sort of mystical experience. All the rational humanism of my childhood was too deeply ingrained for me to make the leap into any sort of altered state of consciousness.

Much to my astonishment, after a few days of seriously trying to follow the exercises, I sensed a change taking place in myself; strange things were happening for which I could not account in my orderly scheme of things. My mind was going out of its head!

Reprinted from *Eda LeShan: On Living Your Life* (New York: Harper and Row, 1982).

Before this seminar began in California, there had been a birthday party for my mother in New York. She's had a heart condition for many years, but on that particular night she seemed especially happy, relaxed and loving. It was therefore a great shock to get a telephone call from my father a day or two later that she was back in the hospital, in great pain—and very frightened. My brother told me that my mother was so agitated and terrified that no amount of medication seemed to be helping—she was moaning and crying, even in her sleep. When I talked to my mother on the phone, however, she assured me there was no reason for returning to New York, that she had had such episodes before, and would recover again.

One of the exercises that Larry uses to help people begin to meditate is to have each member of the group go off by him or herself and for fifteen minutes, simply say his or her own first name over and over again, out loud. The reason for this is that we rarely hear ourselves saying our own names, and it seems to help to break down one's usual way of perceiving the world enough to allow new and different mental experiences to occur.* It was easy, in a beautiful forest setting, for each of us to find a place to be alone, and Larry moved from one to another to see how we were doing.

I sat down on a tree stump, closed my eyes and began saying, "Eda, Eda," over and over again, feeling how strange that sounded. After a while—I had no idea how much time had passed—Larry said it was about ten or fifteen minutes—something really weird began to happen to me. I felt as if I was moving away from the sense of being an individual sitting on a log, and that I was suddenly moving out into space—that I had become part of the total universe and that that was a safe and wonderful place to be—almost like one tiny star in a great galaxy. My first thought was that I would never again be frightened of dying, that I felt so much part of a larger universe that I could never feel lost and alone, but rather was connected forever to everything.

*This can be a very upsetting meditation. I would not recommend it to anyone who does not have serious experience in meditation or who is not doing it under supervision.—LL

I thought of my mother and wished in a deeper way than ever before that somehow I could share this moment with her—that *I was with her*, and that I wanted her to feel what I was feeling—this sense of deep inner peace, the Oneness with a kind of universal ALL in which she and I could never be separated, and in which there was such serenity and awe and peace.

I burst into tears. Larry appeared, and we sat quietly, and I told him what had happened to me. The exercise had taken me out of my ordinary sense of myself—I had, much to my surprise, discovered an alternative state of consciousness.

Later that day my father called to tell me my mother had died and I flew back to New York. After the funeral, at my parents' apartment, I was helping others to put some food on the dining room table, when I heard my aunt telling a story to some other relatives. She was saying that my mother, in spite of the enormous amounts of medication she was getting, had been moaning and tossing restlessly, when suddenly she sat straight up in bed and said in a clear and quiet voice, "Oh, it's so peaceful here in the forest!" She lay back in bed and slept—and died soon thereafter.

Some time later, Larry and I figured out the time difference between New York and California, and realized that the episode my aunt had described occurred at the time I had been in the altered state of consciousness.

4

✦

Designing a Science of Psychical Research

The sciences that have been able to make definite progress in the past have followed courses containing similar steps and procedures. These have included the selection of a specific domain, the identification and definition of the observables in this domain, and a concentration on the question of the relationships between these observables.[1] In the history of psychical research, it was not believed possible to do this with certain types of data. These types included the meaningful, "need-determined" psi occurrences.

To begin the approach we are suggesting here, let us decide on the "domain" with which most psychical research is concerned. This is the cross-section of experience in which more than one human being is involved. Simply put, it is in this domain that we *observe* psi occurrences. Furthermore, although it appears possible to conceive of pure clairvoyance or precognition in a one-person cosmos, this calls for a great deal of intellectual stretching. More important, however, is the fact that it is almost impossible to conceive of a person, a human being, developing or existing as such alone in the universe. If, as the psychologist W. Köhler once wrote, "A solitary chimpanzee is not a chimpanzee," how much more is this

Much of the following chapter was written in collaboration with the physicist-philosopher Henry Margenau. —LL true of a solitary human being? A voluminous literature in psychology and psychiatry bears clear witness that human psychological characteristics develop only in the working-out of relationships with other persons.[2]

In this domain of multiple human beings, we find three classes of observables: *self-aware individual identity, communication,* and *relationships between people.* There may well be other observables we will wish to include later, but these will suffice at this time. If we want to follow the classical model of the successful sciences, our primary question will be: How do these observables relate to one another? Along the course of this exploration, we will find ways to define our terms carefully. However, for the purpose of demonstrating the possibility of this scientific model for psychical research, we can at present be content with doing this in a general and rather loose way. *Communication* we will define for now as the detectable transmission of information between two individuals. We shall divide this into two kinds: sensory communication, in which the transmission takes place through the sensory organs or through manipulation of information that was acquired through them; and nonsensory communication, or psi occurrences. We are (following Charles Honorton) inserting a "detectable" into both these definitions, since nondetectable entities or processes are of no interest to science. It may well be, for example, that psi transmission of information always or usually accompanies sensory transmission of the identical information. If true, however, this would not be detectable, and science takes it as a general operating rule that entities that are in principle not detectable are to be treated as if they do not exist. (Compare the history of the concept of the "ether" in nineteenth-century physics.)

Psi occurrences are detectable only when sensory communication between those involved is blocked. (Otherwise, whether or not psi is occurring, one attributes the communication to the sensory interaction.) For our purposes, then, psi occurs when sensory communication is blocked. Since our interest here is in the "need-determined" type of occurrence, there obviously must also be a need to communicate on the part of at least one of the persons involved.

Let us now begin to make hypotheses about the connections among these three observables—communication, relationships, and identity. So far as communication is concerned, we are interested, as already indicated, in the type that occurs when information transmission through sensory systems is blocked and there is a need to communicate. Such communications—Ehrenwald's "need-determined" type—are of events important to at least one of the individuals concerned.

Let us look first at the observable *relationship*. Do we already know anything about this that can be of help in formulating testable hypotheses? It turns out that there is a good deal that we already know. From the research by psychologists into small-group behavior—for example, from the Group Dynamics of Kurt Lewin and his students and from the Interaction Process Analysis of Robert F. Bales and his followers—we can make some definite statements. (It should be borne in mind that the "small group" starts with and includes the dyad—two people relating to each other.)

There is, for example, a measurable attribute in relationships generally called "cohesion." This has been defined as "the total field or forces which acts on members to remain in a group"[3]—or, in a dyad, to continue the relationship. (An observable in science may have attributes, as the observable "force" in physics has the attributes of strength, as measured in number of dynes, and direction. Cohesion is analogous to the attribute "strength of force" in physics.)

Using cohesion as the primary variable, the following conditions (secondary observables) are among those that have been shown to affect it:

1. Cohesion is greater when the emphasis in the group has been on cooperation rather than competition.
2. Cohesion is greater in a democratically organized group than in a group governed by authoritarian or laissez-faire procedures.

Our first hypothesis then might be that *psi occurrences are more frequent between individuals whose relationships have been cooperative than they are between individuals whose relationships have been competitive.* Our second hypothesis might be that *psi occurrences are more frequent in egalitarian than in authoritarian groups.* (Although testing these hypotheses would be difficult and require various correction factors for bias, the tests themselves are perfectly feasible.)

Since the stronger the interpersonal attractions among its members, the greater the group cohesion,[4] we can make a third hypothesis: *Psi occurrences are more frequent between people who like each other than between people who do not.* (A study by Carl Sargent has shown that parapsychologists who get good experimental results are more likely to be open, warm, and friendly than those who do not.)[5]

Social class in the United States is a system that tends to separate individuals into different groups, lifestyles, and patterns, and an individual's position in the social-class structure is generally determinable. We might therefore make this hypothesis: *Psi occurrences between two members of different social classes will be reported much less frequently than between members of the same social class.* (This, however, will not be true if there exists a special group that includes both of them and is important to at least one of them.) The implication of these two hypotheses for the psychological design of psi experiments and laboratory behavior of staff is obvious.

The social psychologist Robert F. Bales and others of his school have approached communication primarily from the viewpoint of problem-solving activity. They have demonstrated, for example, in a large number of experiments that human beings need and strive for stability (another attribute of the observable relationship) in their dealings with others and develop roles to maintain this stability. Solutions to problems of interaction become institutionalized as roles so that stability (and therefore predictability) can exist. (There are, of course, other reasons for the development of roles.) Bales has demonstrated the consistency and importance of this aspect of relationships.[6]

A role can be approached from both a sociological aspect ("He is a father to those children") and from a psychological aspect ("He is a very demanding father"). There is a strong tendency for roles in a group (including a dyad) to be consistent and communications to be relevant to them. We might therefore make the following hypothesis: *A psi occurrence will be in keeping both sociologically and psychologically with the role that the "agent" plays or has played in relation to the "percipient."* A second hypothesis might be that *psi occurrences are more likely when the stability of an important relationship is threatened and communication is necessary to maintain it, but sensory modes of communication are blocked.*

In his work, Bales has developed a method of analyzing verbal communications in a relationship into four general classes: positive reactions; attempted answers; questions; and negative reactions. The first three classes indicate that the predominant forces operating at this time are those favoring the continuance of the relationship, the fourth favoring its discontinuance. In terms of our earlier comments about cohesion, we might make the hypothesis that *verbal communications preceding psi occurrences are more frequent in the first three classes than in the fourth.*

These hypotheses are concerned with the mutual variations between the observables' relationship (specifically its attributes, cohesion, and stability) and communication. The same type of hypotheses can be made concerning the variation between psi occurrences (the type of communication we are interested in here) and identity.[7]

The interactions between relationship and identity have been widely explored in a large number of contexts within scientific, artistic, and literary frameworks. It has long been clear that one cannot exist without the other, and it does not seem necessary here to describe the large body of literature that is unanimous on this point.[8] Further, it has become clear that although there may be shorter or longer periods in the individual's life when direct communication is cut off (the Robinson Crusoe situation, for example), the three observables of identity, communication, and relationship are as interdependent as are volume, pressure, and temperature in another domain. Without identity I cannot relate. There cannot be a *yes* unless there is also the possibility of a *no*. It is the consciousness of a relationship or membership in a group that is important in determining identity and behavior. As M. S. Olmstead noted, "Groups have a consciousness of membership which may, indeed, persist even when intercourse with co-members has ceased, as with an Englishman living abroad."[9]

Let us here use as one aspect of the observable "identity" Erik Erickson's definition that identity is the ability to maintain important patterns in the face of change.[10]

Since the evidence from the literature is clear that people strive to maintain their identity with the same intensity and need as they do to maintain their relationships, we can make certain hypotheses about the interaction of identity and the frequency of psi occurrence. One example of this would be as follows: *The psi occurrence tends to aid the individual in maintaining important patterns in the face of change.* Restated, this hypothesis would read: *Psi occurrences tend to stabilize identity and maintain consistency of action and perception more often than they tend to destabilize identity.*

All the hypotheses we have presented here seem to have much in common. This is because we are dealing with a gestalt[11] of identity, communication, and relationships, and making it possible to test the hypotheses. Ernst Cassirer has pointed out, for example, that a major function of language is to ensure that a group has a common experience of reality and that the participants are enabled to communicate, relate, and maintain their identities.[12]

Certainly much work in this area has already been done. There have been a good number of studies examining the relationships of the small, flaw-determined psi occurrences (card guessing and working with random-number generators) to variables such as liking and disliking the experimenter, democratic and authoritarian settings for the study, belief in ESP, and so forth. These have been done by some of the best researchers in the field, such as Gertrude Schmeidler, Rhea White, Carl Sargent, and Charles Honorton. However, it needs to be done in a systematic way, starting with a summary of what we know and do not know. Also, most importantly, we need to include the larger, need-determined occurrences.

This is all very well, but for a deeper understanding of psi we have to go beyond the assets and limitations of this kind of science.

There are at least two basic models for scientific methodology. For the study of psi, we need both. The model I have described so far in this chapter is valid and necessary for psychical and parapsychological research, but we also need the other if we are going to get far in our endeavors.

The model presented in the first part of this chapter is designed for, and only applicable to, domains and observables that are quantifiable in nature. But we are primarily here dealing with consciousness, and consciousness is not quantifiable. This is partly because there is only private access to our inner life, and for something to be quantifiable, there must be public access. More than one of us must be able to view the observables involved. Mary, Sue, and Shirley can all see the table and agree or disagree on its length, and if they disagree they can agree on a method of measuring it and quantify it. In the early twentieth century, psychologists made major attempts to quantify aspects of consciousness. They got as far as naming units of various emotions (such as *romeos* for units of love) before they gave the whole thing up. They realized that if Mary says, "I have two 'dols' [from *dolor*] of pain in my toothache," or if Sue says, "I feel three 'exuberants' of joy in seeing you again," there is no possible way Shirley can attach a number to either of these conditions, because the units of measure are so personal and subjective. She can make a "guesstimate" as to how strong they are, but that is about all.

For consciousness and other nonquantifiable observables, we also need the other model of science. And its rules, procedures, and areas of applicability have long been worked out.

It is always hard to see one's own assumptions, and harder still to see that they are limited in scope or inapplicable in *this* situation. The assumptions that a science inevitably leads to quantification of material, general laws covering the entire field, and precise prediction of the behavior of individual entities are so deeply ingrained in our thinking that they have been almost unquestionable. Only very slowly have we begun to realize that they were largely inapplicable to a science of human consciousness and only applicable to part of a science of the paranormal.

Although it has taken us a long time to see the problem, it was investigated in detail at the end of the nineteenth century. It had started with Giambattista Vico's earlier studies of the field of history and the necessary methodology for it. Later Wilhelm Dilthey, Heinrich Rickett, and Wilhelm Windelband generalized this problem to the social sciences in general and to psychology in particular. There were various names for the two very different scientific methods that gradually emerged as essential. The French philosopher Ernest Renan called them *la science de la nature* and *la science de l'humanité*. The nineteenth-century German philosopher Wilhelm Dilthey called them *Naturwissenschaft* and *Geisteswissenschaft*—roughly translated, "science of nature" and "science of the spirit" respectively. Another nineteenth-century German philosopher, Wilhelm Windelband (and later Gordon Allport), called them "nomothetic" and "idiographic" science. Despite the different names, there was strong agreement as to the structure and methods necessary for this *science de l'humanité*, the science of human consciousness—and of psi.

In three separate fields of the social sciences—ethology (the study of organisms in their natural environment), history, and dynamic psychology—we see the new science of human consciousness being widely used. (It is also used with precision and excellence by good nursery school teachers!) Curiously, we find one specific individual close to the beginning of its use in all three disciplines. Windelband was a friend of Freud, who revolutionized psychology. Konrad Lorenz described Windelband's influence on the new field of ethology. The British philosopher R. G. Collingwood wrote of his importance to the field of history. Although Windelband is little known today, this important philosopher had an amazing effect on the social sciences.

Idiographic science, which is necessary to the sciences of human consciousness and of psi, does not have or seek general laws. It does have a clear method. In it, one starts from the specific. I examine a person suffering from schizophrenia. I try to learn as much about this person as I can, to comprehend him on as many levels as possible. I ask, Who is this person? Who is this schizophrenic? What is a schizophrenic? How does this schizophrenic differ from others I put in the same category? I do not arrive at any laws carved in stone. I can never make exact predictions about the behavior of specific schizophrenics. But as I proceed, my understanding deepens. I learn more about what it is and feels like to be a schizophrenic. A way to help people with this illness emerges. I can know more about what they see and how they perceive the world to which they are responding. My "understanding" becomes a "standing under" the same sky and in the same world. It takes training, hard work, and disciplined subjectivity to do this. It is as rigorous a scientific path as is that of *la science de la nature*.

The situation is the same if instead of examining a schizophrenic, I examine a large-scale psi event. I ask, What is this event? What is a psi event? How does this psi event differ from others? I arrive at no general laws. I do arrive at a deeper understanding of psi.

In the first part of this chapter, I have shown how large-scale psi events can be dealt with by nomothetic science, the "science of nature." But this is not enough. For the study of psi we need both methods. Need-determined psi is primarily and most often a matter of consciousness. And for the study of consciousness, we need idiographic science, the "science of the spirit." We need both if we are to make any real progress in understanding the paranormal.

The most widely studied case history in all the social sciences is Freud's 1905 study "Fragment of an Analysis of a Case of Hysteria" ("Dora"). This was the first detailed publication of the new science of psychoanalysis and the new concepts that revolutionized psychology. In this beautiful and immensely influential paper, Freud shows this method in detail. Who is Dora? What are the observables? What is a hysteric? How does this hysteric differ from other hysterics? How is she similar? No general laws emerge, nor does the paper enable us to make specific clinical predictions, but after reading the paper, we understand much more about hysteria than we did before. Our *comprehension* is deepened, and when we see the next individual with this type of personality, organization, and problems, we will understand more and have a better sense of how to try to help. Furthermore, our comprehension of what it is to be human will be more profound. It is this method, idiographic science, *la science de l'humanité*, that is primarily appropriate and relevant to the study of nonquantitative, everything-connected-to-everything-else, space-is-not-an-observable, never-exactly-the-same-twice consciousness, and to the study of psi events.

An example is the Hinchliffe case, which I described at the beginning of chapter 1. What is this psi event? It is Colonel Henderson's perception of Hinchliffe. What is a psi event? It is an event in which someone shows clear evidence of having information that he could not have obtained through the senses. How does this psi event differ from others? There is the intense desperation of Hinchliffe as he realized he and his passenger were completely lost. There was the perception of this by another, highly experienced pilot whom he knew (possibly an ex-superior officer). Can we feel our way into the situation, feel Hinchliffe's need to get help ("Hendy, I'm lost. What am I going to do? I'm lost, I'm lost"), and the impossibility of any communication in those days when airplanes did not carry radios? Let us empathize with Hinchliffe (and with his passenger). What about Henderson? He is called "Hendy." Does that mean anything about their previous relationship? Is it relevant that he was also at sea? Had he, as seems likely from his rank, been previously in the role of taking care of other pilots? Can we empathize with him? This is a holistic approach to the psi event. It will not lead us to any laws or predictive techniques. But as we continue this idiographic approach, we will develop more and more of a "comprehension" of psi, a feeling for variables, a sense of what it is all about. That, combined with the data from nomothetic science, will, hopefully, lead us in the direction we wish to go.

This is how I would learn about painting and music. It is how I would learn about religious experience, love, grief, creative expression, courage and steadfastness in the face of adversity, or any of the other important or meaningful parts of human life. And by "important" I mean as lived and defined by human beings, not as defined by a theoretical model. "Important" includes what we hold in common with the rest of the animal life on this planet—our need to survive as individuals and as a species. It also includes what we have by virtue of being human: our psychological and spiritual needs; our need to create beauty; our compassion; our hopes and fears and aspirations; our ability to design utopias for all and to build concentration camps for many; our Saint Teresas, Beethovens, Tamerlanes, and Hitlers; our ability to experience the emotions so perfectly captured by Elizabeth Barrett Browning when she writes:

> I love thee to the depth and breadth and height
> My soul can reach, when feeling out of sight
> For the ends of Being and ideal grace.
> I love thee to the level of every day's
> Most quiet need, by sun and candle-light.[13]

The laboratory and *la science de la nature* have very real and important roles to play in our attempt to learn about and to comprehend ourselves. The laboratory is an absolutely necessary place for testing hypotheses and ideas arrived at through other means. As insights emerge, they must be put to proof in the laboratory, which thus becomes an integral part of our scientific endeavor to find out who we are and where we are going. Kept in its place, the experimental method and the laboratory are irreplaceable parts of our science; used exclusively, as they have often been in psychology and psychical research, they spell disaster.

A type of psi occurrence that can be studied by both scientific methods is psychic healing. This phenomenon is one in which the "healer" goes through certain mental and emotional procedures (sometimes accompanied by physical movements such as the laying-on of hands) and the "healee" sometimes shows positive, though medically unpredictable, changes.

Groups of patients have been studied with the approach of nomothetic science (*la méthode de la nature*). With this approach, experiments have included animals such as mice that have been anesthetized; the experimental groups received healing and the control groups did not. Judged by the standard of getting up on all four legs, the experimental groups recovered faster than the control groups to a strongly statistical level. Another experiment involved mice that received (under anesthetic) a standard wound in the back. Here, too, the experimental groups recovered at a faster rate.

The experimental approach has included human "healees" who received treatments at a distance at times unknown to them. Other designs have been used, including with plants and with experimental groups that did not know they were being healed. The standards of these studies have been very high. They have included two Ph.D. dissertations (by Joyce Goodrich and Shirley Winston) with carefully chosen control groups, random-number tables, and the full ruling-out of suggestion, the placebo effect, and inadequate statistics. The studies done using this approach have shown beyond question to anyone who reads the literature that the phenomenon exists.

Individual cases have been studied with the idiographic method (*la science de l'humanité*), just as Freud worked with "Dora" to learn more about hysterics and about the human condition. This approach has taught us much about the experience of both healer and healee and about the conditions that help the healer achieve the emotional and intellectual state that we believe furthers the functioning of psi. We have learned how to teach most individuals (at any rate the highly skewed group who come to us to learn) how to achieve this state in seminars of under a week.[14]

There is no contradiction between the facts that psi has uncovered and the facts found in the study of other segments of reality. They may be very different, but they are compatible. They do not contradict each other because they apply to different domains.

In 1979, physicist Henry Margenau and I sent a letter to *Science* expressing the view that psychic phenomena could be and have been studied scientifically, and that the available data not only contradicted no basic scientific laws but strongly deserved consideration from science today. The letter was rejected because "it put the burden of proof on the critics of parapsychology rather than on its supporters." This objection was completely irrelevant to the letter, which I reproduce below.

> It appears to be a matter of common sense to any scientifically trained person today that ESP (telepathy, clairvoyance, precognition) is impossible, since such phenomena—if they existed—would violate known and proven scientific laws. On this basis we can confidently predict that reports of occurrences of this kind are due to poor observation, bad experimental design, or outright chicanery. Old wives' tales and pretentious occultism, even if dressed up in pseudo-experimental designs, do not belong in scientific journals unless studied as psychological and anthropological phenomena.
>
> This is the attitude of many scientists and appears to most of us to be completely reasonable. Further, there is little question that a goodly number, at least, of reports of ESP are due to the above-mentioned infelicities.
>
> However, a question can be raised as to exactly what scientific laws would be violated by the occurrence of ESP. We have assumed that they are of the stature of the law of conservation of energy and momentum, the second law of thermodynamics, the principle of causality and the exclusion principle of quantum mechanics. When we examine scientific laws of this caliber, however, we find them unrelated to the existence or non-existence of ESP.
>
> Further as concerns conservation of energy, physics itself tolerates curious exceptions, or at any rate, it considers phenomena which alter the usual conception of this basic principle. The equivalence of mass and energy modifies its classical meaning: the need for introducing "negative kinetic energy states" together with holes in their distribution which represent particles, extends its scope immensely and dilutes its meaning. Electrons can pass through barriers in a way which energy conservation in old-style physics would not have permitted and in the quantum theory of scattering one is forced to introduce "virtual states" which violate it.
>
> It is indeed questionable that ESP strains the energy conservation principle even as much as these innovations do, for it is not at

all certain that the transmission of information must be identified with that of energy or mass.

Does ESP violate the canon against "action-at-a-distance"? Perhaps it would if there were such a universal principle. There are current, at present, respectable conjectures among physicists who introduce massless fields in which phenomena can be transmitted instantly. In quantum mechanics a debate is raging about non-locality of interactions: the term is a high-brow version of action-at-a-distance which is believed by some serious theorists to be required in order to solve the EPR paradox. ESP is not stranger than some of the discussions in this field.

The limiting character of the speed of light is violated by new, speculative entities (tachyons) whose existence seems to be suggested by a reasonable interpretation of relativity theory.

Strangely it does not seem possible to find the scientific laws or principles violated by the existence of ESP. We *can* find contradictions between ESP and our culturally accepted view of reality, but not—as many of us have believed—between ESP and the scientific laws that have been so laboriously developed. Unless we find such contradictions, it may be advisable to look more carefully at reports of these strange and uncomfortable phenomena which come to us from trained scientists and fulfill the basic rules of scientific research. We believe the number of these high quality reports is already considerable and increasing.

Case History

"A Transatlantic 'Chair Test'"
Aristide H. Esser and Lawrence LeShan

Center for the Study of Psychic Phenomena
at the Rockland State Hospital, Orangeburg, N.Y.

For many years the Dutch sensitive Gerard Croiset has given evidence of his ability for psi-cognition in so-called "chair tests." Mr. Croiset's procedure has been designed by him and Professor W. H. C. Tenhaeff, Director of the Parapsychology Institute of the State University of Utrecht, to ensure that precognitive material cannot possibly be either fraudulently prepared or tampered with after preparation. The simple routine is that Mr. Croiset gives a "reading" for a person who will be present at a future public meeting, identifying that person only by the seat he will occupy in the auditorium. The record is mailed in advance to someone who has no connection with the meeting, and who is required to deliver this record to the meeting organizer, after the meeting has started. The audience selects seats by freechoice as they enter. Even if they know a "chair test" is to be made, no one there could know which chair Croiset had selected. Usually, however, the audience does not know of the test until after the meeting has started. The meeting organizer, once the meeting has begun, asks the people present to remain seated after the meeting has come to an end to witness the results of an experiment.

Although many such tests have been performed in Europe, the first opportunity to conduct one with an American audience came when LL was asked to present his work to a meeting at the Research Center at Rockland State Hospital. Among the people invited to this meeting was local resident, Mrs. Suhm, who, like AHE, knew Croiset and suggested that this opportunity be taken for a chair test. AHE, on June

Reprinted from *Journal of the Society for Psychical Research* 45 (no. 742, December 1969): 169-70.

11, telephoned Croiset, who immediately agreed to hold a witnessed session at his house in Utrecht, Holland. This session on June 12, 1968 was recorded on film and audio tape; the records were then sent to Dr. Nathan S. Kline, Director of Research at Rockland State Hospital, who would not be attending the meeting scheduled for June 21, 1968. Dr. Kline instructed his secretary to bring these records to AHE at the conclusion of the meeting at which LL would speak. The meeting started at 2:00 p.m., with AHE asking all present to remain for an unscheduled event following the lecture and the question and answer period. Of the 25–30 people present, almost all remained seated, and at 3:00 p.m. Dr. Kline's secretary brought in the letter and sound tape containing Mr. Croiset's predictions. We were prepared to record the chair test for Mr. Croiset with 8 mm black and white film and audio tape. AHE now told the audience of Mr. Croiset's letter containing information on one of the persons present and that it was our intention to record the reactions of this person and of the audience to the reading of this written material. AHE then opened the letter and translated it from the Dutch language.

The material dealt with the person sitting in the second row third from the left as seen from the speaker's rostrum. This person turned out to be Mr. M., a member of our research Center Staff. Mr. Croiset made thirteen statements which were specific enough so that their validity could be checked. These statements, the actual situation, and the reactions from the audience are presented below.

1. "In the second row, third chair from the left, there will be a gentleman, middle aged, firmly built, his white shirt very clearly visible and he has sparse bristly hair." Mr. M., who was seated in his chair is thirty-three years old, weighs 210 pounds, and wore a white shirt (he was the only one in the audience who had taken off his coat, and the shirt was conspicuous); his hair was wavy and long. He stated, however, that he "used to have" a crew cut. In our opinion, Mr. M. can fairly be described as "firmly built." He gives the impression of being muscular rather than overweight.

2. "Has he tried one of these days to pry loose a string from a package with his fingers, and has he hurt his finger doing this?" No.

3. "Has he tried to open with a pen a piece of copper tubing that was plugged?" No. However, Miss RS, who sat in the next row of chairs behind Mr. M., had just been doing this with the plastic tubing of an aquarium aerator, which was dirty with green algae and resembled an oxidized copper tube.

4. "Has he tried to bury a piece of paper or to attach it to a fence in the garden . . . with emotion . . . something special that he would not do otherwise?" No. However, the before mentioned Miss RS had been trying to apply tar paper to the bottom of her garden fence to keep the weeds down during the previous weekend.

5. "If he is home . . . does he see (from his window) a street corner with a shop, with an awning?" No.

6. ". . . live with three persons, but also with seven persons at home?" Yes, Mr. M. lives with three persons in his rented apartment; and he is the oldest son in a family of seven, where he still often visits.

7. "Has he had recently a severe pain in his right shin?" Yes. Mr. M. suffers from a slipped disk which gave him pain specifically in the lower right leg, around the shin area. No one else in the audience admitted to a similar experience.

8. "Has he recently laughed heartily about a drum band in which a fellow with the big drum made a funny movement?" Yes. Mr. M. remembered vividly this detail from the movie "Charlie Bubbles." This is a current movie which, at the time of the experiment, was playing theatres in the area of the Center. No one else in the audience admitted to a similar experience.

9. "I see at the moment a kind of Chinese house . . . he has entered and had to remove his shoes, which has occasioned some commotion. It is like a temple with two pillars . . . an oriental home . . . He did not like to do this." Mr. M. immediately remembered just within the past week having visited the apartment of an Indian doctor, who had asked him to remove his shoes before entering. The doctor had installed two spring-loaded floor-to-ceiling posts for ornamental reasons. No one else in the audience had visited this home at the time of the meeting.

10. ". . . had he in an emotional upset torn up a map? There was present a lady behind a desk . . . in a kind of study where on the side two gentlemen were seated." No.

11. "This gentleman is too old to build sand castles, but has he put sand in a pot . . . I do not understand it." No. However, Mr. M. said he had recently been toying with a very fine long silver chain, which he put into a coffee mug to pour onto the table in an effort to make designs.

12. "Has he recently been involved with a person where between the toes a sharp object had come . . . one toe was hurt and had to be bandaged?" A qualified yes, within the past week an aunt of Mr. M.'s fiancée had been operated for a disfigured toe. This lady had shown him the bandaged toe, and they had discussed the operation.

13. "I see momentarily a street, people, a man with a briefcase and another person trying to tear this briefcase loose . . . had this happened to him personally or will this story emotionally be related to him . . . which can happen between this moment . . . and the time of the chair test?" No. However, a Mr. S. who had also been at the meeting came later to AHE to tell that such an embarrassing scene had been related to him by his father within the past week and that he had been ashamed to tell this to the audience.

Afterwards, two additional data were revealed. Mr. M. had not known about the meeting until three minutes before it started and had never been to a discussion of psi before; neither did he have any interest in the subject. Also Mr. M. tries mostly to sit somewhat apart from others in an audience; and in retrospect he could not explain to himself his sitting conspicuously in the second row. In his words, "I felt more or less compelled when I came in the room to sit in that seat."

In summary, six of Croiset's statements about the person he had perceived as sitting in the chair applied directly to Mr. M. One of them, the statement about the oriental home, is astonishingly specific and did not apply to anyone else in the audience. Obviously, some statements were of a more general nature, and others could be construed to apply to one other man or to one woman in the audience. Nevertheless, the cumulative probabilities of anybody's predicting such personal events are exceedingly small if the following considerations are taken into account:

1. The subject did not have any interest in parapsychology and did not know about the meeting in advance.
2. Almost half of the statements about this subject were true.
3. One of the statements made could only have been true for this subject in this audience.

60

The tapes and films, both of Mr. Croiset's witnessed session on June 12, 1968, in Utrecht, and of the meeting on June 21, 1968, at Rockland State Hospital, are on file at the Center for the Study of Psychic Phenomena and are available to qualified persons for research purposes.

Comment by Lawrence LeShan: I have included this experiment in precognition in full here partly as an example of the kind of clues it provides, clues which, if taken with other data from other incidents, may help to further our understanding.

There were real and unmistakable "hits" that applied only to the person sitting in the chair that Croiset had specified. These included the conspicuous white shirt (this man was the only one present who had removed his jacket), the "pain in the right shin," the "Charlie Bubbles" incident, and the "oriental house" prediction. If statistical analysis techniques applied to data of this sort (they do not, but that does not stop people from trying), the odds against these correlations would be so astronomical as to be ridiculous.

Then there were predictions that applied to the person sitting in the chair behind the chosen subject. These must be counted as "misses" (a psi prediction is either correct or not), but they provide materials from which we may be able to learn. The "qualified misses" (such as #12) and the full misses (such as #2 and #5) also furnish data for our analysis.

We need to approach the data provided in this sort of study in two ways, first from *la méthode de l'humanité*: idiographic science.[15] What is a paranormal event? What is *this* paranormal event? How does it differ from other such events? How is it similar? We are not searching for general laws, but for comprehension.

Second, we must approach the data from the viewpoint of *la méthode de la nature*: nomothetic science. This is the classical scientific method. Are there aspects of the observables that we have found which can be generalized, quantified, developed into general laws? Can we measure the frequency of certain patterns and relationships? What predictions can we learn to make? While we have not been able to do these things in the study of consciousness, we must try to do them in the study of psi.

Neither of these two approaches owns the new territory we are exploring. We must try both with equally open hearts and minds. (The old wisdom is that the laboratory is an essential tool for testing hypotheses we have framed outside of the laboratory. This may or may not be true for a science of psi.) One other reason for including this experiment is that it is a pure and tight example of precognition—the most difficult type of psi for many people to accept. The data were recorded and witnessed on June 12. At that time there was no possible way of predicting who would sit in which chair on June 21 through the channel of sense or by extrapolating from information gained through the senses. And yet specific statements were made and recorded, and some of them were accurate in a way that excludes chance.

There are only three choices here: (1) to ignore the data so that you can remain comfortable with your cultural assumptions about the nature of reality; (2) to assume that the authors of this article and/or the witnesses of the event were deliberately lying; or (3) to accept that this is a genuine case of precognition and set out on a journey from there. The first two choices are, for most people, the most comfortable.[16]

5

Psi and
Altered States of Consciousness

It is of course the merest truism that all our experimental knowledge and our understanding of nature is impossible and nonexistent apart from our mental processes.

—P. W. Bridgman

It is the theory which decides what we can observe.

—Albert Einstein

Whatever is fact was first in theory.

—Johann Wolfgang von Goethe

Impossible events do not occur. Therefore, if a scientist is faced with the fact that an impossible event has occurred—our daily fare as psychical researchers—the paradox must be resolved. This can be done only by redefining reality in such a way that what was previously impossible now becomes possible. If the theory must bow to the brute fact, we must be clear as to what is the theory and what is the fact. The paranormal event is the fact. Our definition of *reality*, which decides for us what is possible and what is impossible, is the theory.

This is an absolutely critical point in the study of the paranormal. The question is, where do we get our knowledge of what is possible, and what is impossible and therefore "paranormal"? We have largely ignored the point that a definition of *paranormal* comes from a definition of *reality* and that such a definition is a theory, not a fact.

If, along with most critics and debunkers of the paranormal, we were to accept that our definition of reality is a fact and that we *know* what reality is and how it works, we would be holding a view that would make both science and philosophy tautological, as they are both disciplines that question and explore reality. Technology uses common sense; it accepts a particular view of reality and does the best it can with that view to accomplish our ends. Science, as Robert Oppenheimer once put it, uses uncommon sense; it is a search for new definitions and understandings. Technology takes the locally accepted definition of reality as a fact; science takes it as a theory.

The kind of uncommon sense, of daring and questioning of basic definitions that is needed in science, the kind we need in psychical and parapsychological research, is shown by a remark of the great mathematician David Hilbert. He had once mentioned a new student of his who seemed to show great promise. Sometime later the philosopher Ernst Cassirer asked him what had happened to this student. Hilbert replied, "Oh, he did not have enough imagination to be a mathematician, so he became a poet!"

As students of psi, we have tended to hold our imaginations in check and to accept the common, everyday definition of reality that made the facts we observed in our work impossible. We have kept trying to show that these facts occurred anyway, and when we tried to explain *how* they occurred, we generally tried to find the explanation within the commonsense definition. Only occasionally have we been aware that this definition was a theory, not a fact.

The eighteenth-century philosopher David Hume was in error in his famous argument on disbelief in miracles. Hume pointed out that since a psi event was a violation of the laws of reality and therefore was highly improbable, it was much more likely that the reporter was mistaken or lied than that the event occurred. Which, asked Hume, is more probable, that a miracle happened or that the report of it was false? Hume's error lay in defining his interpretation of how the world works as a fact when it was a theory. As a *fact*, it was blatantly impossible for it to be contradicted by another fact (the miracle). Therefore the paranormal occurrence logically never happened, and the observers *were* mistaken or lying. The chain of logic is unassailable so long as the definition remains unquestioned. Once the definition is examined, however, it becomes clear that it is a theory, not a fact, and therefore that when opposed by a fact, it must be given up as inaccurate or incomplete.

We can see the problem clearly when we think about the colleagues of Galileo who refused to look through the telescope. They refused because they thought it unnecessary to look; they had confused their theory about reality with facts. As far as they were concerned, they knew the facts, and there was simply no point in observing a contradictory fact; the telescope's view was necessarily false, as it contradicted known facts. At this distance we can see their confusion clearly. But it is harder to see the confusion of modern scientists who dismiss the facts of psi as necessarily false since (to their mind, at any rate) the psi facts contradict other known "facts" (which are in reality only a theory). The scientists are as confused as were Galileo's contemporaries, but the scientists' error is a lot harder to see close up.

A theory about reality, a conception of how the world works, that is so real to us that we perceive and react as if it were true, as if it were a fact, can be described in two ways. From one viewpoint, the one we have when we are *using* the theory personally, it is a state of consciousness, and we are responding to the truth about reality. This is how things are. From the other viewpoint, it is simply an integrated set of hypotheses concerning reality and is judged by its effectiveness in attaining whatever goals seem relevant to whoever is doing the judging. It is a theory of metaphysics to be compared with other theories of the same kind.

These two descriptions—a state of consciousness and a metaphysical theory—are the opposite sides of the same coin. When using them, we are talking about the same thing from two different angles. They are the same phenomenon experienced in two different ways.

This has definite implications. It indicates that there is no such thing as a generally "correct" or "normal" state of consciousness, but various states, various organizations of consciousness, that can be compared in the way they succeed in enabling us to solve our problems and arrive at our goals.

What are the problems? What are the goals? In a dream, we operate according to a specific and coherent metaphysical theory; we are in a specific state of consciousness that is different from our ordinary, twenty-first-century Western state of consciousness (the state we generally consider the "normal" or "correct" one). Dreaming is necessary for us; we suffer negative personality changes when it is prevented. Dreaming helps us attain some goal that we can apparently not attain (at least as well) in other known states of consciousness. We have thus two states of consciousness, waking and dreaming, each appropriate to certain of our human goals. Mystics train themselves to attain still other states and believe that these are also essential to full human development, to meeting certain human needs.

From the viewpoint of modern science, physicists take the other side of the mystics' coin. Physicists believe that certain theories about reality are necessary to solve certain problems, and other theories are necessary to solve other problems. The physicists' theories are certainly related to and compatible with each other. For all the relations between the theories about reality that physicists posit as necessary, however, the theories are very different and have very different entities and laws in them. (They demand very different states of consciousness to respond experientially to them.) What is possible in one metaphysical theory is impossible—paranormal—in another. I might point out, for example, that what is perfectly normal on a subatomic level—for an electron to jump from one "orbit" to another without crossing the intervening space—is teleportation on a molecular level. Yet teleportation is generally regarded as paranormal. The theories about reality that physicists posit and use in these two domains are extremely different.

We could find many similar examples. For example, the fact that an electron can pass through two separate holes of a plate at the same time without splitting is perfectly normal in the theory used to deal with problems on a quantum level. But according to the theory used in everyday life, this is bilocation—a paranormal phenomenon. Or in another theory about reality, the one used by the relativity physicist, we have the normal phenomena of event A occurring before event B from the viewpoint of one observer, the two occurring at the same time from the viewpoint of a second observer, and event A occurring after event B from the viewpoint of a third observer. For many events, it is impossible to say whether they occurred simultaneously or in sequence. From the commonsense, everyday theory about reality, this would lead to precognition and retrocognition—paranormal phenomena. The theories about reality that physicists find it necessary to use are so different from the everyday view of reality that what is impossible and paranormal in one frequently is perfectly possible and normal in another.

Even when the same words are used to describe events within different metaphysical systems, they are no more than inviting booby traps, since their meaning is completely different. We learn that an "electron" has "spin." "Spin," we know, is the movement an object describes on itself like the rotation of a planet upon its axis. It is a simple, familiar concept, and we have all seen tops spinning away and understand the term. We come to the clear and intuitive belief that an electron is a small, round object that spins rapidly as it moves. But then we find out that in whatever position the observer places himself or herself, he or she is always in line with the axis of rotation of the spin. It becomes clear that the word *spin* has acquired a completely new meaning in this system. We also find that our small, round object can have no color or absence of color and that it cannot have a temperature. It becomes obvious to us that our intuitive understanding bears no relationship to the actual phenomenon of an electron. We have interpreted events and terms from one metaphysical system, one way of construing reality in terms of another and, following this invalid procedure, have arrived at complete confusion.

We are led here to a revolutionary understanding: a number of metaphysical systems—states of consciousness—are equally valid in an overall sense. None is closer to any "true reality" than any other, and, if it were, we should never have a way of knowing this, because all we can ever perceive is reality *after* it has been construed and shaped by our consciousness, after Edmund Husserl's "enormous a priori of the objective-logical level." The question, Which metaphysical theory is true? is a vacuous one. It can *never* be answered. A question we can deal with, however, is, What can we accomplish with one metaphysical theory, and what can we accomplish with another? Henry Margenau stated this clearly: "The question then, is not whether matter is continuous but how theories succeed when they regard as a continuum the construct which they take to be their system."[1]

The same thing is true of the other side of the coin. We no longer ask, Which state of consciousness is the correct one in that, when using it, we are perceiving and reacting to reality? We can only ask which state of consciousness is most effective in helping us attain which goals. The concept of a "correct" or "normal" state of consciousness is one we will have to put on the crowded and dusty shelf marked, "Outmoded ideas: ingest at your own risk." We can, however, ask, Which state of consciousness is statistically most prevalent in which cultural situations?

These realizations constitute the most staggering and least understood insight of modern science: We are no longer searching for what reality *is*, but rather for ways of usefully construing it, ways of defining it that will help us achieve our goals. There is no "right" metaphysical system, but only a number of systems of limited usefulness, and different segments of reality need different metaphysical systems to make the data from them coherent. There is no "correct" state of consciousness that will reflect "reality," but only a number of states that are useful or useless for specific human purposes.

The next step follows naturally. If there are a number of different, equally "right" metaphysical systems—states of consciousness—and these are quite different in the entities and laws they contain, we can do certain things with some of them that we cannot do in others. What is "paranormal" in a particular construction of reality means that it is forbidden by the basic limiting principles of that construction, and it does not happen when we are using that construction. It cannot be explained by that metaphysical theory since, according to that theory, it does not happen. One cannot explain events within a metaphysical system (a theory about reality) in which they are impossible.

This *must* be kept clear. It is central to the problem we psychical researchers have had in explaining or understanding psi phenomena. If a system of reality-ordering forbids certain events from occurring (such as, in our everyday system, an effect preceding its cause in time), you cannot explain that event within the system. It is like trying to explain parallel lines meeting within the system of Euclidean geometry. You can try all you want to do it, but you simply can't, since one fundamental axiom of Euclidean geometry is that parallel lines never meet, even if extended infinitely. You can explain the convergence of parallel lines by using the system of Riemannian geometry, but you cannot explain it with the Euclidean system. It is not that it is difficult or complex to explain; it simply cannot be done. If an effect appears to precede its cause (as in precognition), you simply have to explain it within a system in which it *can* occur.

There is an old story about the lost traveler who asked a countryman how to get to Salisbury. The farmer replied, "You go north five miles and then turn west . . . No, that's no good. You go west three miles and take the first road north . . . No, that won't do it. You go east and then . . . By God, you can't get there from here!" Parapsychological researchers have tried and tried to get from here to there on the ostensibly solid roads of our ordinary theory about reality. It can't be done. In our ordinary construing of reality, we can do certain things and we can't do others. We can travel to Yankee Stadium, Waterloo Station, or the Place d'Étoile. We can't travel to the day before yesterday or to the Land of Oz. You can perceive something with your senses or extrapolate from known data. You can't be clairvoyant or precognitive. That's just the way things are, and we are going to have to learn to live with it. We need to listen to Thomas Carlyle's response when he heard Margaret Fuller's bravura statement, "I accept the universe." Carlyle replied: "Madame, you'd better."

From this viewpoint, the spiritualists and theologians were more correct than the scientists when they tried to explain paranormal events by saying that spirits produced them or that God produced them. They were taking entities from another metaphysical system to explain phenomena that you can't explain in this one. They were thereby implying that what you needed for the explanation of paranormal events was a different metaphysical system, a different state of consciousness, while scientists tried to hold on to the usual metaphysical system and explain these events in it. Unfortunately, in terms of the usual system, the events were impossible, and therefore their explanations were impossible as well.

I say that the spiritualists and theologians were "more correct" than we were, not that they were "correct." The situation is similar to that of the little boy who came home and told his mother he had gotten first prize in an examination. The question asked had been, "How many legs does a horse have?" He had answered, "Three." When his mother asked how he had gotten the first prize, he replied that all the other children had said, "Two."

If an event is a major violation of our theory about reality, a major revision of that theory is necessary. The scope of the revision has to be related to the scope of the violation. If the violation does not touch basic limiting principles, only minor changes may be indicated. The inverse square law (that the intensity of energy measured by a constant instrument from a source declines by the square of the distance between the measuring instrument and the source) can be modified when we invent the laser or when we differentiate between the intensity of a signal and the amount of information carried by it. The law remains valid on the whole, even though its domain has been reduced.

We need here to find out what sort of position our data force us into. Is it that only a small modification is necessary, as in the case of the laser and the inverse square law? Or is a larger modification necessary, one that will say, in effect, that the old basic structuring of reality remains true and valid, but its domain is now seen as limited, and different laws apply in certain other domains? This is what happened to Newtonian mechanics after the Einsteinian revolution. It is also what happened to Euclidean geometry after N. I. Lobachevsky and Bernhard Riemann devised their non-Euclidean geometries. Euclidean geometry is still valid, but its domain has been reduced. Other equally valid geometries with different axioms and theorems apply in other segments of reality and are necessary to solve other problems. In Euclidean geometry, a straight line is the shortest distance between two points. In other geometries, it is not.

What sort of revision do psi events require us to make in our theories about reality? The revision must include the fact that our usual commonsense theory about reality is valid in large and important domains. We operate too effectively in most cases, predict too well what effects will follow from what causes, to suspect that our usual theory is totally invalid. We must beware of babies and bathwaters. Our views about reality have not been lightly arrived at and cannot be lightly discarded. The problem does not demand that we throw out our basic theory about reality, but rather that we find out how much we must reduce its domain and devise a theory to fit the new as well as the old data.

We must beware of solipsism as well. (This is the belief that I am the only person in the universe and the creator of everything and everyone in it.) A woman once came up to Bertrand Russell after a talk he gave and told him that she was glad that he was a solipsist because she was one too, and she hoped there were a lot more of them! We can construe reality in a variety of ways, organize, perceive, and react to it according to a number of different patterns, but we are still construing, organizing, perceiving, reacting to *something*. Something is "there." There is more than just "me." The something is mysterious and, in principle, unknowable in any ultimate sense, but it is real and will only bend in a number of ways in our attempts to organize it into useful patterns. What the laws and limits of this bending are, we do not yet know, but we can be sure that they exist. We cannot make the universe into anything we wish; we can only organize it into a number of functional patterns. If there are 437 schizophrenics in a mental hospital, this does not mean that there are 437 legitimate and valid ways of organizing reality. It means only that there are 437 schizophrenics in the hospital.

Perhaps we must ultimately come to an understanding of reality similar to the one we reached in the "nature–nurture" controversy regarding the development of personality. After a long period of insisting that it was nearly all nature or nearly all nurture, we have come to the conclusion that nature sets the outside limits of possibility, but within these the individual person is such a combination of both that we can never separate out how much each has played in forming the end product, in forming the person at the time we are examining him or her.

The twentieth-century Indian philosopher Sarvepalli Radhakrishnan stated this viewpoint clearly in his *Eastern Religions and Western Thought*: "The objective world exists. It is not an illusion. It is real not in being ultimate, but in being a form, an expression of the ultimate. To regard the world as ultimately real is delusion."[2]

The only way out of the predicament posed by the occurrence of psi events is to say that our usual theory about reality is valid, but that there is *more*. Our usual theory applies in certain situations (which includes most of our practical life, tying our shoelaces and buying airplane tickets and designing the shoes and the airplanes), but there are other situations this theory cannot deal with. In science, we are used to this procedure. We no longer try to predict the behavior of subatomic particles using the same cause-and-effect theories with which we predict the behavior of molar masses moving (relative to us) at speeds of a few dozen or a few hundred miles per hour. We have not thrown out our usual concepts of what reality is and how it works, but rather we have limited them to a more restricted domain. We have said, in effect: They are true and valid, but there is more. And the *more* is very different.

Paranormal means "impossible" by the laws of a particular system of construing reality in terms of our usual *theory* about what reality is. Part of this theory is the axiom that it is the only valid theory. As we have seen, we have had to give this up in many areas, to limit its domain. Instead of continuing to say, This is the true way reality is and works; it is the only valid theory and all other ways are insane, we now say, This is a fruitful way to construe large parts of reality—by and large the parts that are accessible to our ordinary senses—and it is also isomorphic (having the same structure and dynamics) to a state of consciousness that enables us to achieve many of our physical goals.

Faced with the paranormal events that simply could not happen in our usual metaphysical system, we are forced to limit the domain of this system. We have done this elsewhere in science; we must do it with psi events. There is simply nothing else to do, nowhere else to go. *Impossible events do not happen.* If they do, then your definition of *impossible* (and therefore your theory of reality that gives you that definition) is wrong. Wriggle as you like, you can't get away from that—and, God only knows, psychical and parapsychological researchers have tried.

With psi, we have demonstrated the occurrence of "impossible" events. We can now do one of two things. We can change our definitions of what are possible and impossible (and this can be done only by limiting the domain of our usual definition of reality), or we can go right on proving the existence of these events. Maybe if we go on proving them long enough, someone else will point out to us that they inexorably indicate that our usual theory of reality must be limited in its validity. Maybe this outside person will even do our work for us by showing us where and how it is limited. Or we can do the job demanded of us by our science and explore the limitations of that science while developing the alternative metaphysical system we need to explain our data. This will necessarily lead us to exploring *the state of awareness needed to permit psi events to occur,* and we might finally arrive at a coherent and acceptable field of science. We psychical researchers have kept demanding (unsuccessfully) that nonbelievers in psi shift their approach and start believing in impossible facts. Perhaps our real task is to shift our own approach so as to make the impossible facts

73

possible and therefore believable. We can do this only by exploring and changing the definition of reality that decides what is possible and what is impossible.

The only groups that have accepted the idea that you have to change the system of reality ordering you are using if you wish to solve certain problems are physicists and mathematicians. They have overcome some apparently insuperable obstacles in this way. We students of psi have problems that appear to be every bit as impossible as the ones they faced; we can learn from their example.

If we seriously go forward to determine what new organizations of reality are demanded by our psi data, we must expect to have to break with established ideas and with beliefs that have seemed self-evident. There are no sacred cows in real science, and almost every idea that human beings have, in the past, believed to be a basic truth about reality has been overthrown. Up to the twentieth century, for example, nearly every model of the universe had as a cornerstone the axiom *Natura non facit saltus*: there are no leaps in nature. This view is now regarded as false: Both quantum theory in physics and contemporary evolutionary biology require precisely such leaps to account for the phenomena in their respective realms. There is, indeed, no greater bigotry and rigidity of mind than the demand that all possible knowledge be of the same type as that with which we are already familiar, and that explanations on the horizons of our present-day knowledge have in them only the structure and elements familiar in our everyday experience.[3]

There is a large but generally ignored sign over the doorway that all must pass who wish to enter the cathedral of science. The sign reads:

DANGEROUS AND UNSTABLE STRUCTURE.

UNDERGOING MAJOR RENOVATION.

MAY BE TORN DOWN AT ANY MOMENT FOR COMPLETE REBUILDING.

Petrarch, at the beginning of the Renaissance, wrote: "Do not believe the common statement that there is nothing new under the sun and that nothing new can be said. True, Solomon and Terence said that; but since their time, how much is new?"

If this were true in Petrarch's time, how much more true is it in ours?

During a talk he was giving about grace and transcendence, the philosopher Gabriel Marcel was asked to define his terms. He replied, "I see I cannot define it in your terms, gentlemen. But if I had a piano here I could play it for you."

What can be explained in one conception of reality, one world-picture, cannot in another. And no one world-picture has a monopoly on truth. None owns all the territory. From a scientific viewpoint, the question, What is the structure and dynamic of reality? is an invalid one, since it cannot in principle be answered in such a way that the answer can be tested for validity.

Wilhelm Windelband, who contributed so much to the perspective that I am outlining here and to its implication of the necessity of different scientific methods for answering problems in different world-pictures, wrote:

> Thus there is a metaphysic of the nursery and the fairy tale, a metaphysic of practical life, a philosophy of religious doctrine, a conception of life which we enjoy in the work of the poet or artist and seek to assimilate. Each of these varieties . . . [has] its natural, personal, historical assumptions and its usefulness is accordingly limited.[4]

In what world-picture *can* psi events occur without running afoul of its laws, its basic limiting principles? How can we do science in that realm of experience? What are its implications for human beings, for our relationships with ourselves and others and with the cosmos? These are questions raised by the existence of psi events, and these are the ones we must begin to explore.

The next two psi incidents have been included to give some of the flavor of the early days of research in psi. Then the studies were often of mediumistic utterances, automatic writing, and "physical mediumship," the affecting of matter by psychic means. The first incident presented here, "Mrs. Verrall," was done in 1912; the second, The Four Photographs, in the 1970s, but they both are typical of the work done in the last quarter of the nineteenth century and the first quarter of the twentieth. The Hinchliffe case presented at the beginning of chapter 1 is also typical of this period.

Case History

"Mrs. Verrall"
Nandor Fodor

One of the older psychic incidents may help in developing a sense of the wide range of the field. An Englishwoman named Margaret Verrall (1851–1912) was one of the most talented and carefully studied sensitives of all time. Her probity and meticulous recording were never questioned, even by the very skeptical members of the Committee of the Society for Psychical Research, who examined and tested her in detail.

In her daily journal for December 11, 1911, Mrs. Verrall recorded the following paranormal perception:

> The cold was intense and a single candle gave poor light. He was lying on the sofa or on a bed and was reading Marmontel by the light of a single candle. . . . The book was lent to him, it did not belong to him. [On Dec. 17 she continued the note.] The name Marmontel is correct. . . . A French book, I think his memoirs. The name of Passy may help him to remember. Passy or Fleury. The book was bound in two volumes, the binding was old and the book was lent to him. The name Marmontel is not on the cover.

On March 1, 1912, Mrs. Verrall was told by a friend, Mr. Marsh, that he read the memoirs of Marmontel on bitterly cold nights in Paris on February 20 and 21, 1912, by the light of a candle. Once he was in bed, another time he reclined on two chairs. He had borrowed the book (it had three volumes), and on February 21 he had read the chapter in which the finding of a picture painted at Passy is described by Marmontel, the discovery being associated with a Mr. Fleury.

Reprinted from Nandor Fodor, *The Encyclopedia of Psychic Science* (New York: University Books, 1966), 352.

Case History

The Four Photographs
Lawrence LeShan

One afternoon in the mid-1970s, I was sitting with Mrs. Garrett (whom we have already met in connection with the Carrington case described in chapter 1) in her office, and we were talking about some papers by the psychiatrist Jules Eisenbud that had recently been published. They concerned a subject of his who could apparently affect unexposed film in a camera. Mrs. Garrett said she would like to try to do this. (To my knowledge, she had never before worked in the field of psychokinesis, that is, mind affecting matter.) I agreed to help, and the next day came to her office by appointment, bringing with me a woman who was working as a professional photographer. She had a camera of the kind in which, after you press the button and expose the film, the film comes out of the bottom a few moments later, and the picture develops as you watch. Mrs. Garrett was busy with some papers on her desk and had completely lost interest in the proposed project. I introduced her to the camera expert and reminded her of our discussion. She said she was too busy and told us to forget it. I protested that we had gone to a good deal of trouble to set it up. She answered, rather angrily, "All right, I'll influence films 1, 3, 5, and 7. Now, I really am busy."

The photographer and I left and went into an empty room in the office. There, after making sure that the dust cap over the lens was still taped firmly in place, she pressed the button that opened the lens, waited until the film had emerged, and did it again and again until all the photos were lying face up on the table.

As they developed, we saw that all except four were completely black. Each of these four had four or five white circles ranging in diameter from an eighth- to a half-inch.

Looking a bit frightened, the photographer turned the four photos over so we could read the numbers painted on their backs. They were 1, 3, 5, and 7. I then witnessed something I have read about but have only seen that one time. I had read the expression, "The blood drained out of her face." But there it was. As if you had opened a spigot at the bottom of her chin, starting from her eye level, her face became absolutely white until there was absolutely no color in it.

6

✦

The Next Step:
Implications of the New Science

It is never necessary to replicate an exact and adequately observed fact.

—Claude Bernard

For better or worse, this is a scientific culture. We listen to religious leaders, gurus, and politicians, but the people we believe speak real truth are the scientists. If they tell us that the universe started with a big bang, that there are black holes that swallow everything around them and constantly grow bigger and bigger, that there is now a period of global warming that we ourselves have instigated, we believe them. We accept that what they work on and agree on is fact.

Think what it would mean if we knew that the people we respect the most were seriously working on mediumistic utterances and emergency clairvoyance, if we knew that government research centers and Rockefeller, Harvard, and Stanford universities were studying deathbed apparitions.

Shortly it would be common knowledge—of the sort we mean when we use the phrase "everybody knows"—that there was more to the human being than is shown by the senses and that we are not permanently stuck inside our own skins.

Just as in the early days of electricity, when scientists first told us that there really was this strange force that would pick up lint if you rubbed a glass rod with flannel, that made the lightning, that would shock you and maybe kill you if it got out of hand, there would be experimenters and speculators all over the place. We would quickly get over the idea that psi could only be explained either by supernatural forces and beings or by the push-pull mechanics of our sensory world. And shortly we would get over the Enlightenment idea that everything—locomotives and butterflies and love and electrons and the human response to kittens and poltergeist activity—worked by the same set of principles. The fruitless quest for simplicity would be over; we would all realize that different segments of reality work on different principles and obey different laws, and that human consciousness and psi obey a different set of laws than does the body. And we would soon find that there are Nikola Teslas and Albert Einsteins of psi out there waiting for the culture to turn them loose.

As a matter of fact, we *have* learned this, but because these discoveries had to do with segments of reality that were not personally or emotionally meaningful, we have not felt that they made any real difference. We have been told—and have intellectually accepted—that there is cause and effect in the sensory world, but not in the microcosm, the quantum world. We have been told that parallel lines never meet in the world of our senses, but do in the macrocosm, the world of relativity, and in this segment of reality the faster you go, the bigger you get and the slower your wristwatch goes. But these facts have not really touched us. They do not pose a threat to the everyday world of our senses. The walls of our lives do not come tumbling down. I go on as I was before, after I learn that the apparently solid desk I lean on is just an empty space with areas of mass, charge, and velocity racing around in it—that it is composed of, in Werner Heisenberg's phrase, "empty space haunted by singularities."

But we are frightened of psi. We push it away. We have known for a hundred years now that most people who have had large-scale psi experiences either forget them as the years go by or else let all the feeling, the emotional connection, drain away in their minds until these memories are in black and white instead of the living color they were in shortly after they happened. And we resolutely do not let the experiences in, do not let them fully affect us.

My wife Eda's mother had had a favorite color that she wore a great deal of the time. The grandchildren (who called her "Granjean") called it "Granjean Blue." About six months after her mother's death, Eda and I were standing in front of our (very small) garden on Cape Cod watching the sunset. Eda was feeling very sad and talked about how deeply she missed her mother and how she wished there would be some sort of sign that there was something more after death, that her mother still somehow existed. I put my arms around her and we stood there while the sun went down. We were feeling a profound sense of loss.

The next morning I went outside early, holding my first cup of coffee. What I saw made me go back to the door and yell for her to come. There in the garden were seven fully mature and blooming plants of a kind we had never seen on Cape Cod before. They were grape arbutus and were of the exact color of "Granjean Blue."

We were both startled and moved, "filled with a wild surmise." However, three weeks later when I asked Eda if this experience had made any difference in her belief systems, she said that they had not.

We reject psi and do not let it become a part of our lives. We forget our own psi experiences and/or the emotions connected to them. They are not a part of our collective worldview. They are not common sense (which Einstein once defined as "that collection of prejudices you have accumulated by age eighteen"). They are impossible in our culturally accepted worldview, and so they create a sort of cognitive dissonance, a contradiction in our perception of what is happening. We automatically tend to reject this conflict. It is unpleasant for us. Unless we can wall the experiences off by considering them as "bubbles of mystery floating around in an otherwise normal universe" and so dismiss their importance, we tend to forget them or our emotional reactions to them. In the latter case there is a marked tendency among many people to deny their possible existence.

Anyone who publishes an account of "debunking" a reported psi event can depend on wide reporting and acceptance. Anyone who publishes (or tries to publish) an account of a clear psi event can depend on the opposite.

There is a widespread idea that if a stage conjuror can produce a particular type of apparent psi, this means that all cases of this type are produced by conjuring. This argument against the existence of psi is frequently used, even when there were no conjurors around when the event happened. From a logical point of view, one might just as well say that because there are counterfeit ten dollar bills in circulation, there are no valid ten dollar bills.

The overall data in this field are made harder to evaluate by the fact that negative results are often not published, but the same thing is true of positive results. The metabolism test results on Mrs. Garrett when she was in the "normal" state and when she was speaking as one of her spirit controls were so markedly different that they were never published, and the experimenter refused to release the raw data.[1]

Some years ago, when I was studying psychic healing, I set up a study with a chemistry professor at Columbia University. The question was whether I could, at a distance, affect the measurements carried out on solutions of water with various kinds of salts dissolved in them. I went into the laboratory where the apparatus was to be set up only once before the study actually started and never entered the building again. From my office several hundred yards away, every day for a week at a specified time, I attempted to "heal" the solutions. Measurements were made before and after. At the end of the week, the professor told me that the results were clearly significant, but if they were published, it would permanently ruin his career. He stopped the experiment and refused to let me have the data. The biochemist Justa Smith reported an almost identical experience.[2]

Nevertheless, the examples given in this book (and thousands more in the professional journals of psi) are real. If you are going to work in a scientific manner, there are many things you must know.

Among these are that you cannot ignore real data no matter how uncomfortable it makes you, that theory must bow to fact, and that one white crow proves that not all crows are black. (And in the published data of psi, we have flocks and flocks of white crows!)

We reject the meaningful existence of psi and, following the world-picture of our society, do not let it become a part of our lives.

However we change in this culture, we follow after science without much or any anxiety, no matter what the changes are. In the last fifty years we have changed from a society whose members found it difficult and requiring careful planning to communicate with others at a distance to the modern cell-phone era where you have only to reach into your pocket to talk to almost anyone. We have moved from a pre-Freud era, a time when the existence of unconscious elements in the mind was unknown, to a post-Freud period. We have moved from an era in which a major problem was to find information to one in which the problem is to keep from being buried in information. We have accepted atomic weapons and global warming, all these and many others, with a basic feeling of stability and safety—at least in terms of what constitutes "reality" and "common sense"—because we are following and are in tune with mainline science.

Elizabeth Mayer, in her book *Extraordinary Knowing,* clearly demonstrates that this is a time of major opportunity for bringing mainline science into the field of psychical research. She details incident after incident in which her psychiatric and psychoanalytic colleagues related psi experiences that had happened to them personally. They talked to her because she managed to convince them that it was safe to do so. They had not told other colleagues about it or published the data because of a very valid fear of destroying their careers. Psi is officially and publicly declared to be impossible in the sciences at the same time that a large percentage of individual scientists believe in it. In a survey of more than 1,100 college professors in the United States, 55 percent of natural scientists, 66 percent of social scientists (psychologists excluded), and 77 percent of academics in the arts, humanities, and education reported believing that psi is either an established fact or a likely possibility. Curiously, the comparable figure for psychologists is 34 percent, and the same number—34 percent—believed it to be a frank impossibility, a view espoused by only 2 percent of the other respondents.[3]

In this respect, it is startling to realize how little our society has changed in the last century or so. In 1926 the psychologist William McDougall wrote, "In that highly educated, skeptical and scientific class, the medical men, it is I think, true to say that about one in three believes that he has firsthand knowledge of it [psi]. And its existence is formally and strongly denied by the professional organizations."[4]

In the same year, the psychiatrist Walter Franklin Prince wrote:

I have noticed that if a small group of intelligent men, not supposed to be impressed by psychical research, get together and such matters are mentioned, and all feel that they are in safe and sane company, usually about half of them begin to relate exceptions. That is to say, man after man opens a little residual closet and takes out some incident which happened to him or to some member of his family, or to some friend whom he trusts, and which he thinks odd and extremely puzzling. I made a remark of this kind once with six men of high standing in various professions. No sooner had I ceased speaking when a physicist whose name is known over the world told of something which had happened to him when a young man—how he heard his father's voice pronouncing his name at the very hour, as it afterwards proved, when his father had died, hundreds of miles away. He ended, "That is something I never could understand." I do not think the physicist would forgive me if I revealed his name. Then, to my equal surprise, a very prominent physician, whose name is familiar to the profession all over the country, told stories of what seemed like telepathy in his own family. A noted editor and a well-known lawyer followed suit.[5]

This is a time of extraordinary potential for bringing mainline science into the study of psi. It is up to those already working in the field to make it happen.

Psychical researchers and parapsychologists will reply to this, "Well and good. You are probably correct. But how do you persuade mainline science to work in this area? We have been trying for over a hundred years with very little success. Do you really think that you suddenly have the answer to the problem we have struggled with so long and hard?" No, I have not come up with an answer, but it is there before us. Let us students of psi start acting like scientists, doing what scientists actually do, not what they say (and frequently believe) that they do. Here are some suggestions:

1. Get over the idea that science is only a matter of controlled experiments done in a laboratory. Geology, astronomy, anthropology, and ethology gave up this belief, and they seem to be doing quite well. Science is not a matter of statistics and control groups. These are sometimes relevant and sometimes not. Science is an unusually obstinate attempt to think clearly about a subject and to study it with the relevant methodology.

2. Get over the Enlightenment idea that all the universe is rational and that there is only one meaning to that word and that everything works on the same principles. This idea has bitten much more deeply into our culture than is generally realized. No one objected very strongly when Hegel wrote, "The real is rational and the rational is real." We must get over the idea that we know how things basically work and that therefore there are no astonishing surprises in store for us. We must give up this concept as Max Planck did when he studied the quantum segment or Einstein did when he studied the macrocosm. Both made progress by allowing themselves to be surprised.

3. Stop trying to prove the existence of psi and get on with studying its properties. If someone does not believe the proofs already published, he or she is not going to believe new ones. You have to go another route. In his "Auguries of Innocence," William Blake wrote:

> He who does not believe what he sees
> Will ne'er believe, do what you please.

4. Stop trying to define psi, and start studying its relationships to other observables. Even if we cannot precisely say what gravity *is*, we can explore its relationships to masses and distances. A favorite story of Henry Margenau was that of the professor who asked a student, "What is electricity?" The student replied, "I forget." The professor said, "Oh, my God! The only man in the world who knew, and he has forgotten!"

5. Stop running away from your major data. Instead, concentrate on learning how to study them scientifically. *Anything* can be studied scientifically if you realize that the white coat, laboratory, and controlled experiments and statistics are simply tools that apply to the study of some areas of reality and not to others. (I am repeating this point because so many scientists regard the controlled experiment as a sacred icon that must not be questioned. I once wrote in a scientific journal that the experimental method had limitations. The letters that the editor and I received could not have been more vituperative if I had stated that the writers' mothers rented themselves by the hour and their sisters gave green stamps.)

6. Psi researchers *must* stop going around with long faces and feelings of inferiority because they have not been able to come up with a "repeatable experiment," at least not with large-scale, need-determined events. The phrase "repeatable experiments" has a fine ring, and scientists tend to throw it around as if they were talking about the Holy Grail. However, there are fields of science in which it simply does not apply, and psi research with large-scale, need-determined events is one of them. A repeatable experiment in this field is a psi-producing machine, and you are simply not going to get such a machine relating to any of the important aspects of human consciousness. You are not going to get a love-producing machine or a creativity-producing machine, nor are you going to produce love at will in a laboratory. Just as you are not going to get a repeatable experiment in astronomy, history, or oceanography, you are

not going to get it in psi.[6] Why? Because the basic idea of controlled experiments is that you vary one thing and hold everything else steady. Except for the variable you are changing, everything else remains the same (*ceteris paribus*—"all else being equal"). Consciousness, however, is never the same twice. William James wrote that the idea of the same situation existing in consciousness at two different moments is "as mythical as the Jack of Spades." And, whatever else we find out about psi, it *does* involve consciousness.

7. Parapsychological researchers studying the large, meaningful cases should not be thrown off course when they hear the word *anecdotal*. In practice this term has come to mean, "I do not like the idea of the existence of the event. It makes me uncomfortable. Let us forget it and say it is not scientific, as it has no statistics attached to it." Nevertheless, an event occurred or it did not occur; statistics do not change this. If the event is one that the person is comfortable with, he will call it a "case presentation" and refer to it approvingly from time to time. If not, he will dismiss it as "anecdotal." A datum—such as a large-scale psi event of the sort I have been discussing throughout this work—either occurred or did not occur, and labeling it is not going to change that fact. If the event is one that is impossible under your theory of how reality is and works, then it is a "white crow," which, as William James observed, proves all crows are not black. In this case, you have two basic choices. You can hold onto your theory about reality and declare that the event did not occur since it *could* not occur. Here the fact has bowed to your theory, and your magical thinking and deductive logic keep you comfortable. Or you can say that your theory of how reality works is invalid or limited in scope and must be revised in terms of the fact that the event occurred. This is thinking scientifically. In the first case, you are stating that you know so much about reality that it holds no more surprises for you, and that all new

facts, if they are real, are of the same order as the ones with which you are familiar.

St. Augustine observed, "There are no miracles which violate the laws of nature. There are only events which violate our limited knowledge of the laws of nature." Psychical researchers should keep this in mind when they are told that psi events are impossible and therefore did not occur. Like David Hume, they are confusing their theory about reality with facts. And in science we need to be clear about which is the theory and which is the fact that violates it, and that in science the theory must *always* bow to the fact.

8. Psi researchers must stop seeing themselves as somehow inferior to scientists in other fields. Our standards of research—under the intense pressure and rejection that has long been directed against us—are as high and often higher than those of the "hard" sciences such as physics and chemistry. Our data are as tight as theirs, and if mainline scientists do not accept this fact, we must make it clear that it is due to their ignorance and not to weaknesses in the data or in our methodologies. When we are dismissed by people who have mistaken their theories about reality for facts (and therefore know that psi cannot be real since it contradicts their "facts"), we must avoid being apologetic.

The famous physicist William Barrett once gave a lecture on psychical research to a group of scientific colleagues. At the end a colleague said, "A very interesting lecture, Barrett, but it's all tosh, you know." Barrett replied, "Well, you are a scientific man. When you have spent as many weeks as I have years studying these subjects I shall value your opinion."[7]

As the British philosopher C. D. Broad once observed, the great majority of those who dismiss the field as nonexistent know nothing about the extensive data we have accumulated in the past hundred-plus years and are of the opinion that they know so much about reality that it holds no surprises for them:

Anyone who at the present day expresses confident opinions, whether positive or negative, on ostensibly paranormal phenomena, without making himself thoroughly acquainted with the main methods and results of the careful and long continued work [of psychical research] may be dismissed without further ceremony as a conceited ignoramus.[8]

In short, the best way to get psi research accepted by our culture at large is first to have it accepted by mainline science. And the best way to have it accepted by mainline science is for psi researchers to start acting like scientists and not like poor relations.

Case History

"The Vanished Man:
A Psychometry Experiment
with Mrs. Eileen J. Garrett"
Lawrence LeShan

On the morning of February 24, 1966, Dr. B, a physician, checked into a hotel in a Midwestern city to begin several days of a professional conference. At 5 p.m. that same day he checked out of the hotel and disappeared. His wife became very worried when no word was heard from him and the hotel reported that he had gone without leaving a forwarding address. The police were unable to find anyone who had seen him leave except the hotel clerk. . . .

For two years preceding this date I had been engaged in research with Mrs. Eileen J. Garrett, who is probably the most talented and experienced sensitive engaged in active work today. Mrs. Garrett, who was trained by J. Hewat McKenzie at the British College of Psychic Science, has been taking part in experimental research for many years and her seriousness and ability are attested to by a wide variety of publications dating over a forty-year period.

My wife was a childhood friend of Mrs. B, although she had not seen or corresponded with her in many years, nor has she ever met Dr. B. (I had never met either of them and have not to this day). When in early March, 1966, Mrs. LeShan was on a visit to the distant city where the Bs lived, she decided to telephone them and heard the news of the disappearance. She visited their home, talked with Mrs. B, and suggested that Mrs. Garrett might be of assistance. On her return, Mrs. LeShan told me of Dr. B's disappearance, of his profession, of his wife's distress, and of her suggestion concerning Mrs. Garrett.

This article of mine is reprinted from the *Journal of the American Society for Psychical Research* 62 (no. 1, January 1968). This work was done under the auspices of a grant from Frederick Ayer II.—LL

On March eighteenth I received an envelope from Mrs. B containing a two-inch square of cloth cut from a shirt Dr. B had worn the day before he left for the professional conference. I telephoned Mrs. Garrett at 10 a.m. and asked if she had a few free minutes that day as I had a problem requiring her assistance. An appointment was made for 2 p.m. and I planned to ask her to psychometrize the article in a waking state. On my arrival at the Parapsychology Foundation, however, Mrs. Garrett, with absolutely no discussion at this point, said to set up the tape recorder for a trance sitting. Mrs. Garrett, Mrs. Bethe Pontorno (her executive assistant), and I went to the room used for sittings and started the recorder. (It must be emphasized that Mrs. Garrett's total knowledge of the matter at this point—at least insofar as she might have gained it through normal channels—consisted of my telephoned sentences, "I have a problem requiring your assistance. Do you have a few minutes you could spare today?" Aside from this, I had never discussed the matter with her or with anyone else who could conceivably have been in touch with her.)

A trance sitting was held, recorded by tape and also in shorthand by Mrs. Pontorno. After being greeted by Uvani, Mrs. Garrett's control,* and greeting him, I said, "A man has vanished, disappeared. His wife is very upset and seeks some idea of his whereabouts." Uvani asked if I had something belonging to this man and I gave Mrs. Garrett the square of cloth cut from Dr. B's shirt. After speaking for some time about the man, Uvani stated that the cloth " . . . does not have very much—only his anxiety," and asked for an article such as a pipe or something else he usually carried around with him. The sitting ended at this point. (In spite of Uvani's statement that the cloth "does not have very much," it will be seen from the tabulation below . . . that a good deal of veridical information had been obtained from it.)

Partly because Mrs. Garrett prefers, for research methodology reasons, not to discuss while in the waking state material that has emerged during a trance, and partly because a second exploration with her was

---

*For a discussion of the nature of a "control," see the appendix. —LL

contemplated, she was told after the first sitting only that it had been a "good and useful one" and that another was planned. (After the second and final sitting, she was kept informed of new developments, such as Dr. B's return, as they became known.)

On the evening of March eighteenth, after the first sitting, I telephoned Mrs. B and asked her for an article her husband often carried. She sent me a sealed box which, without knowing what it contained, I sealed inside two heavy Manila envelopes so that no clues could be obtained from the return address. (Later, after the package had been returned unopened to her, Mrs. B stated that it contained one of her husband's favorite pens.) On March 28th, at 10:50 a.m., a second sitting was held with Mrs. Garrett at the Parapsychology Foundation. She spoke about the package for forty minutes, psychometrizing it in a waking state. Her statements were again recorded by tape and in shorthand.

On the same date (March 28th), at 1 p.m. (same time zone as the Parapsychology Foundation), Mrs. B received a letter from her husband from La Jolla stating that he had been ill and would shortly return home. This was the first time she, or the police, had any idea where Dr. B had been, although Mrs. Garrett had said on March eighteenth that he had gone in the direction of California, and on March 28th, before noon, that he was in La Jolla. . . . [See item 92 below.]

One hundred statements which seemed concrete enough to be checked specifically as "right" or "wrong" were taken from the transcripts after the second sitting, numbered, and typed on a separate list. When Dr. B returned home on April 8, 1966, he was sent this list and asked to annotate each statement. He did not return the material until May 25th; unfortunately, by this time he had begun to "cover up" and repress the entire incident of his disappearance. This process is apparent in some of his annotations . . . , which are a fair distance from the truth.

Due to the necessity of disguising the case for publication, the complete annotated transcripts of the two sittings cannot be presented here.[9] However, certain of Mrs. Garrett's statements seem to stand out as clearly indicating her paranormal acquisition of information and these are presented in the tabulation below so that the heart of the reason for considering this case to be evidential may be immediately apparent. . . .

Selected Statements from the 1966 Transcripts

Date	Statements by Mrs. Garrett	Comments by L. LeShan[10]
#13 March 18	I think (that before he left) he has spoken much that he wanted to go to Mexico—is this so?	On this date, this information was not known to Mrs. B, the police, or me. However, after he returned (on April 8, 1966) Mrs. B found in his suitcase a fairly extensive correspondence discussing and planning his trip to Mexico. This correspondence antedated his disappearance and started six months before it. (Information given by Mrs. B on telephone on April 10.)
#16 March 18	I am sure he thought of going to California and then on to Mexico.	Correspondence described in #13 above shows he planned to go to California first and then to Mexico. (On this date, not known to Mrs. B., the police, or me. Information given by Mrs. B on telephone on April 10.)
#25 March 18	Going away was not without premeditation on his part.	As shown by correspondence described in #13, he had been planning this for at least 6 months. Also, 6 months before he had opened a special bank account (unknown to his wife) and withdrew all the money, turning it into traveler's checks, shortly before his disappearance. (Known to me on this date. Mrs. B had been notified by the bank on March 1 that the account had existed and on March 3 she told my wife about it.)

Date	Statements by Mrs. Garrett	Comments by L. LeShan[10]
#55 **March 28**	I get the impression of someone who is in the middle 40s.	Dr. B's age was 42. (Not known to me at this date. However, I would probably have estimated his age to be in the 40s if I had thought about it.)
#57 **March 28**	A man who, as a youngster, was considered to be a prodigy.	On March 3 Mrs. B told my wife that he had been considered a prodigy as a child. (The fact was known to me on this date.)
#59 **March 28** **and #60** **March 28**	Somewhere between the ages of 13 and 15, there was a loss in the family. I believe it was his father.	When he was 14 years old, his father deserted the family and was not heard of again for 25 years. (This was not known to me or to my wife at the time of the sitting. That evening [March 28], in a telephone conversation with Mrs. B, my wife asked her if there had been a "loss in the family" when Dr. B was 13–15 years old, and was given this information.)
#67 **March 28**	(He is) about 5 feet 10.	He is 5 feet 9. (This was not known to me or to my wife at the time of the sitting. It was found in a police "missing persons" circular sent to me by Mrs. B on April 10.)
#85 **March 28**	He has a good psychologist friend.	During Mrs. LeShan's visit to the Bs home on March 3, she was introduced to a man, a psychologist, and his wife, by Mrs. B who said, "These are our closest friends."
#92 **March 28**	I see him at La Jolla.	He spent nearly all the time of his disappearance, except when he was in Mexico, in La Jolla. His first letter home was mailed from there. (This "hit" is a most unusual one. At the time this statement was made neither the police, Mrs. B, nor I had any idea where he was.)

Perhaps the strongest of these evidential statements were Number 92 (that Dr. B was in La Jolla—a statement made at a time when neither Mrs. B, the police, nor I knew where he was) and Numbers 59 and 60 (concerning the loss of his father when he was between the ages of thirteen and fifteen; his father's desertion was known to Mrs. B, but not to me). No matter how the rest of the statements are evaluated, it would seem that these statements clearly indicate paranormal acquisition of information on the part of Mrs. Garrett.

In conclusion, this is a curiously "old-fashioned" article. It does not fit in with the current interests of many researchers and is not embedded in the modern stream of parapsychology. Indeed, there has been such a change in our field since the time when articles like this were commonly seen in the American journals that psychical researcher Jules Eisenbud could recently say to a meeting of the Parapsychological Association that "were William James alive and trying to peddle his remarkable Mrs. Piper among his colleagues today" it is doubtful if he would get very far.[11] No particular disagreement with this statement was voiced from the floor. At present parapsychology stresses statistical evaluations, the effects of hypnosis, reduced sensory input and drugs on paranormal ability, the relationship of personality structure and attitude toward scoring level, and other approaches of this sort. In spite of repeated statements made by speakers at various parapsychology conferences in the past few years that we are hampered by the lack of good sensitives to work with, very little is currently being done with those that are available and willing to take part in research.

Then why publish a paper like this at all? Simply because, articles of faith aside, it is *not* established which approach—the qualitative or the quantitative—will be ultimately more fruitful, which will lend more to the development of understanding in our field.

7

What Dare I Hope?

All the human search for understanding and meaning, wrote the philosopher Immanuel Kant, is contained in four questions:

> What can I know?
> What ought I to do?
> What dare I hope?
> What is a human being?

As the study of psi becomes a mature science and its existence becomes a part of our cultural world-picture, becomes "common sense," what can we legitimately expect to happen? What I dare hope for is a time when psi becomes as widely accepted as was the unconscious after Freud, or global warming after enough scientific research had been done on the subject.

Since this is a scientific and sense-oriented culture, we can be sure that it will not change in the face of the new knowledge in the same way that faith-based medieval society would have changed. We will probably not go back to believing in angels and devils and the whims and battles of good and evil forces. We will move toward the relationships of the appearance of psi to feelings, belief systems, relationships, and other variables we find in the segment (or segments) of reality that we are studying—the other observables. This is valid, whether or not the segment is quantitative. Consciousness is a nonquantitative segment. You cannot assign meaningful numbers to the intensity of emotions, nor can you quantify the distance between a feeling and a memory. We cannot measure in numbers our positive (or negative) reactions to a book by Kipling or Updike (although in another segment, we can accurately compare the number of copies of these books sold in any given year).

Another nonquantitative segment is the world-picture of the myth and fairy tale. The number of miles Orpheus traveled on his trip to the underworld is no more discernible than the number of miles from Munchkinland to the Emerald City. Laws govern consciousness, the fairy tale, and the myth, but they are quite different laws than those that govern the falling of apples and the movements of planets. We can be clear about these different sets of laws and the different ways to truth in the different segments of reality we humans have carved out and in which we live.

We will take the data of psychic research on their own terms and see where they lead. Since we are talking about the acceptance of major personal observables that simply do not fit into our usual view of the world, we can expect major changes in the definition of ourselves as humans and of the world in which we live.

This does not mean we will give up the picture of reality as given by our physical senses. This works far too well for it to be false. If, using it, I set out for Chicago, I arrive in Chicago and not in London, yesterday, or on the deck of Sinbad's ship. Furthermore, the picture revealed by our senses is absolutely necessary for our biological survival.[1] But we did not have to abandon this world-picture when we found that there were very different definitions, laws, and relationships in the microcosm and the macrocosm. Each of these is in a different segment of reality, and different laws apply in different segments. There is no contradiction.

So, after this preamble, what *can* we legitimately expect to happen to us and our society after the existence of large-scale psi events becomes part of the background assumptions in our culture?

1. The view of ourselves and others as locked within our own skins, communicating with others only through physical movements of our body, will be loosened.

2. A new view of "What am I?" and "What are other people?" will become the general cultural concept. This view will be a dual one: seeing ourselves and each other simultaneously as individuals and as part of something larger. This will be close to the concept of most serious esoteric schools and spiritual development groups: that when I see you as an individual in the foreground, in the background is the view of you as a part of something larger (and vice versa).

3. This new concept will affect our behavior. Belief systems are true in their effects. Among these effects will be changes in how we treat ourselves, others, and the planetary nest in which we live.

4. The changes will be large enough and soon enough that they will help move the human race off the Endangered Species List.

It is impossible to predict precisely what these changes would be or how rapidly they would change the society. (It might take a generation raised on these beliefs for their effects to be fully felt.) They are, however, very close to the changes almost universally reported by individuals after a serious mystical experience or after long training in one of the esoteric schools. In general, these include more peace and zest in one's own life and less-conflicted relations with others. They also include a deep sense of our relationship to the earth as a whole.

Contrary to general belief, mystics tend to be unusually efficient at whatever they do. Many Western mystics are noted for their contribution to the arts and sciences, and for being unusually successful in the business world![2]

It is hard to see how these changes would be negative in terms of individual happiness, human relations, or the survival of our species. This is not only because "the truth shall make you free." Nor is it because without recognizing these dimensions of our being, we shall have to keep a large part of our nature repressed, and there is always a high price to pay for doing this. Rather it is that the emphasis on the connectedness of you and me, of each and all of us, should go far in changing our behavior toward ourselves and others in a positive direction.

It is not possible now to say whether the changes I have been talking about would increase the frequency of large-scale psi events, although this seems a likely result. It would certainly increase the ability to evaluate them, to accept them as valid, and to accept their implications. It would certainly increase the frequency of their being reported to others and of being remembered when they happen to you.

Beyond these, the specific changes and beliefs among "mystics" and those who have had a serious mystical experience (such as that reported on page 39 by Eda LeShan) differ widely. The differences seem due more to where you started from than to the experience itself. It seems reasonable to assume that this problem will also be part of the cultural changes I have been writing about.

What dare I hope? That an everyday acceptance of large-scale psi events will lead to personal and cultural changes that will help us overcome the great problems that now threaten to destroy us—that with the new picture of what a human being is, we can learn how to stop killing each other and poisoning our only planet, our nest and home.

That every cultural change that helps solve the immediate problems of the culture eventually brings new and unforeseen problems in its wake is now a truism. But the problems of the future will have to be left to the people of the future. We must deal with ours.

Appendix

"When Is Uvani?"
Lawrence LeShan

The following report is included here not as the definitive solution of a problem in psychical research, but as an example of the kind of thinking "outside the box" that may be necessary in the development of the new science for which we need to account in our data.

In psychical research, there is a strange and recurrent phenomenon. This is the appearance of a class of entities known as "spirit-controls." Typically this phenomenon appears under the following conditions. A person who may or may not have been previously involved in psychical matters suddenly claims—either in words or in writing—to be another personality. This new persona (let us call it a *spirit control*) generally acts in a quite consistent manner from appearance to appearance. The original personality which manifests in the body of the person (let us call this person the *medium*) usually claims that he or she has no knowledge of these events. Either mediums say they were not present or conscious during the episode or else they regard the writing arm as if it were writing under its own volition. The spirit control usually claims to have been alive as a human being in the temporal past. Sometimes this claim can be traced to an actual human being of whom we can find records; sometimes it cannot.

This phenomenon differs from what we call a "multiple personality" in that the medium chooses when it is to appear. Also, competition or conflict between the spirit control and the medium seldom occurs.

Frequently, spirit controls seem to show a very consistent personality over a long period of time. (The records show that "Uvani"—the

"When Is Uvani?" is reprinted from *The Journal of the American Society for Psychical Research*, vol. 89 (April 1995).

leading spirit control of Eileen Garrett—was consistent in personality and philosophic viewpoint for over, at least, a fifty-year period.) Further, the best mediums frequently show strong paranormal abilities in that they often display evidence that they have specific information that they could not have obtained through normal channels of sense or by extrapolating from information gained in this way. The *Journal of the Society for Psychical Research*, for example, has published hundreds of reports of such events. In addition, the mediums with the longest-lasting and most consistent of these spirit controls tend to be healthy personalities.

Research and speculation as to whether this phenomenon was indicative of actual spirit survival of biological death (as the spirit controls insist) or was a phenomenon of a multiple personality type have been less than successful. There has apparently been no way to decide between these two hypotheses. Even Eileen Garrett, the premier medium of her age, who spent most of her adult life searching for the meaning of her mediumship, could come to no conclusion between them. About a year before her death I asked her what she thought of her spirit controls after a half century of experience with them and after having worked on the problem with every serious person she could find. (This list, including Carl Jung, is very long and impressive.) She replied:

> Larry, I have to answer you in what seems to be a light and humorous way, but it's the best I can do! It is as if on Monday, Wednesday and Friday I think that they are spirits as they say, and on Tuesday, Thursday and Saturday I think that they are multiple personality split-offs I have invented in order to make my work easier. And as if on Sunday I try not to think about the problem.

It is, of course, an old faith of science that if serious men and women work seriously for a long time on a question and can come up with no answer or even a theoretical way to find one, they are asking the wrong question. On this basis the question of whether this phenomenon is one of surviving spirits or of personality split-offs is clearly the wrong question. Is there a way we could ask another?

Let us start with the fact that the spirit controls often demonstrate paranormal abilities and have information that they could not
have acquired through normal channels of sense or by extrapolation
from data so gathered. Who doubts that this is so simply has not read
the relevant literature and further discussion with them is not useful
until they do so. In the words of C. D. Broad:

> And anyone who at the present day expresses confident opinions, whether
> positive or negative, on ostensibly paranormal phenomena, without making
> himself thoroughly acquainted with the main methods and results of the
> careful and long-continued work [of Psychical Research] may be dismissed
> without further ceremony as a conceited ignoramus. (Broad, 1926, p. 6)

In all serious cases described as "paranormal," the normal laws of
space and time are violated. We have been unable to "explain" this,
and that has been the central problem of psychical research. We *know*
that these laws of space and time cannot be violated, that exceptions
cannot occur. We also *know* and have clearly and scientifically demonstrated in the laboratory and elsewhere that they are sometimes
broken. In spite of all our efforts we have had to leave them, in Jacob
Needleman's words, as "bubbles of mystery floating around in an otherwise 'normal' universe" (personal communication, 1969).

Is it fruitful to try to approach the paradox in a new way? Let us
try and begin by asking, "Are there classes of things (entities) to which
the normal laws and limitations of space and time apply and classes of
things to which they do not?"

Looked at in this manner it becomes evident that there *are* two
classes of things. The first class we might describe as *structural entities*. These are things with length, breadth, and thickness. They are
always subject to the "normal" laws of space and time. Things of this
sort cannot, for example, move faster than the speed of light. They
have a definite physical existence during their duration—and even as
Bishop Berkeley emphasized—they go on with this existence whether
or not they are at a particular moment in anyone's consciousness. (One
can be hit on the back of the head by a falling meteorite of which no
one—except perhaps God—was aware.) Of this class of things we can

meaningfully ask the question "What is it?" and expect to be able to get a reasonable answer at whatever level the question is put. It is concerning this class of entity that Dean Swift (quoted in Yeats, 1970, p. 4) wrote:

> Matter, as wise logicians say,
> Cannot without form subsist:
> And form, say I as well as they,
> Must fail if matter brings no grist.

The second class of things we might call *functional entities*. These do not have any length, breadth, or thickness. They cannot be detected by any form of instrumentation although their effects often can be. They are not bound by the "normal" laws of space and time and often can, for example, move faster than light. If I point a telescope at the star Aldebaran and then swing it to focus on the star Altair, something very "real," the *point of focus* of the telescope, has moved faster than light. Or, if I take two long rulers laid overlapping with a very narrow angle between them so that at one end they overlap and at the other end there is a small separation, I can locate a definite point of divergence. Then, if I snap the separated ends together, this point of divergence will move along the rulers at a speed (at least theoretically) faster than light. Other examples could be given.

There are curious and difficult entities. In a famous incident, Ludwig Wittgenstein was asked what a mathematical point was since it had no length, breadth, or thickness. He replied, "A mathematical point is a place to start an argument!" In this profound answer Wittgenstein pointed up the functional rather than the structural nature of this entity.

The existence of these entities also differs considerably from that of structural entities. They do not have a continuous existence whether or not they are being mentally conceptualized. Indeed, they fit rather well the formulation that Bishop Berkeley attempted to establish—they exist only when they are held in a mind, only when being conceptualized, only when being considered to exist. There is no reality to a mathematical point unless it is being conceptualized as such. You cannot be affected by the focus of a telescope when no one is thinking of it. Put in a better way, a functional entity can have no effect on other entities (and so—for all intents and purposes—ceases to exist) unless it is being conceptualized as existing.

One of the most useful devices in mathematics is the square root of −1. One would be hard put—or find it impossible—to solve many mathematical and engineering problems without it. Curiously, however, there is no such number as the square root of −1. The square root of 9 is 3, as 3 times 3 equals 9. The square root of 1 is 1, as 1 times 1 is 1. However, there is no number which multiplied by itself is −1.

However, mathematicians saw a need for the square root of minus one. Working within a world picture, a conception of reality that made it possible, they conceptualized it: it then existed as a functional entity—having the same reality as a mathematical point. And the concept has proven itself useful and durable.

Of this class of entities we cannot ask the question "What is it?" and expect a reasonable answer. We can, however, ask other questions such as "When is it?" and hope to obtain a satisfactory reply. (A mathematical point is when it is conceptualized as the intersection of two lines.)

The question "where" a functional entity is "when" it exists cannot always be answered. With some functional entities, as our mathematical point, we can answer it and locate it in both space and time. With others, a melody for example, we cannot answer the question. We can locate the melody in time, when it is being conceptualized, but not in space.

In essence we might say: A functional entity is what it does and when it does it. Further, it only is (does anything) when it is being conceptualized by a perceiving and conscious entity.

Let us pause for a moment and ask about "things" with no length, breadth, and thickness. Can they really exist? Are there really entities about which one cannot successfully ask "what" or sometimes "where," but can, perhaps, ask "when" and "why" and which do not exist between perceptions of them? Mathematical points are all very fine, but are there others more meaningful for our lives?

To the obvious question "Can a functional entity affect a structural entity?" we must answer in the affirmative. A mathematical point has an effect on a surveyor and subsequently on a steam shovel and a railway line. One can be profoundly affected by the point of aim of a hidden person with a rifle!

The essential point of this formulation is that it presents us with two classes of entities, one of which is not bound by the "normal" laws of space and time (that is, it can behave "paranormally") and can affect the other class of entities, which is bound by these laws. Let us explore and see if this will help us deal with the problems of psychical research.

As I pointed out earlier, paranormal events are called paranormal because they appear to be impossible to us. Impossible events do not happen. Once it has been established that a particular impossible event happens, science has devised a method of dealing with the problem. We do not change our definition of reality. Instead we limit the realm in which our definition of reality holds sway. The revolutions led by Planck and Einstein were, in large part, accomplished by limiting Newtonian reality to those realms of experience which could, at least theoretically, be perceived by the senses or by mechanical extensions of the senses. In those realms too small for this type of perception, the rules define quite a different sort of reality. (Specific causation is statistical rather than mechanical, etc.)* In the realm of the too large or fast to be perceived by the channels of sense the basic rules of reality are again changed. (The term simultaneous, for example, drastically changes its meaning with all that this implies.)

In this paper I am suggesting a similar limitation. The common sense rules of reality apply to one class and not to another. They apply

---

*The physicist Erwin Schrodinger (1961, p. 25) expressed this as follows: "As our mental eye penetrates into smaller and smaller distances and shorter and shorter times, we find nature behaving so entirely differently from what we observe in visible and palpable bodies of our surrounding that no model shaped after our large-scale experiences can be true."

to structural entities and not to functional ones. What is normal for one class of entities is paranormal to the other. The limitation "impossible" in the sensory world refers to rules covering only structural entities, not functional ones. Just as it is not paranormal for an electron to pass through two holes in a plate at the same time without splitting (if a human did this we would call it "bilocation" and phone the American Society for Psychical Research!), it is not paranormal for a functional entity to violate the speed of light barrier or, according to its design, violate other rules for defining events as paranormal.

In short, the rules of what is possible and what is impossible, which we so clearly and confidently know, apply to structural entities and not to functional ones. If we then hypothesize that spirit controls are functional entities, the problem of how they produce "impossible paranormal" phenomena vanishes.

Does, for example, a serious spirit control (such as Mrs. Garrett's Uvani, Mrs. Piper's Phinuit, Mrs. Leonard's Feda, or Douglas Johnson's Chang) fill the conditions we know so far which belong to the class of functional entities? Certainly we have never been able to detect any physical structure related to, let us choose, Uvani. He (whatever Uvani turns out to eventually be, the pronoun "he" seems more polite than "it") has beyond a doubt shown the ability to behave paranormally, that is, to acquire information, the possession of which clearly violates the laws of space and time. A typical example of this is given in my paper, "The Vanished Man" (LeShan, 1967). See page 92.

Does Uvani exist between those times at which he is conceptualized as existing? If we take as a gauge of what we mean by "existing" the ability to influence other entities, then Uvani does not exist between conceptualizations. (Modern science takes "detectability" as the criterion for existence. It was by this criterion that the Michelson-Morley experiment is construed as "proving" that the ether does not exist.) When in existence, Uvani can influence the behavior of structural entities such as the medium, the sitter, etc.

Two rather interesting incidents come to mind here. In the first, that very high-level psychic Rosalind Heywood told me of a time when she was talking to Abdul Latif, another major spirit control of Eileen Garrett. She decided to use her own highly developed paranormal abilities to perceive Abdul Latif. She wrote me: "I put out my antennae and it seemed to me that he only existed for the subject under discussion" (Personal communication, 1965).

In the other incident, psychiatrist Ira Progoff asked Uvani while Eileen Garrett was in trance, "How have you been since last we met?" Uvani, an otherwise invariably calm and self-possessed persona, became completely confused and unable to answer the question. In fact, he could not seem to understand it, although he asked Progoff on various other occasions how Progoff had been since last they met and was obviously capable of understanding both the implications of the questions and the answers (Progoff, 1967).

In these incidents, the spirit controls certainly seem to be indicating that they follow the rule of existence of the functional entity—that they exist only when they are conceptualized as existing.

I have elsewhere (LeShan, 1974) described the state of consciousness during which paranormal processes occur, calling this the Clairvoyant Reality. This state of consciousness is particularly oriented to the perception of relationships rather than to the perception of structure. In it, and in the world-picture which it accepts as the valid metaphysical system, relationships are seen as primary and individual structures and the separateness of these structures is seen as secondary or illusory. This same metaphysic is accepted as valid by both the serious mystic and by the Einsteinian physicist. Thus we might quote Arthur Eddington to the effect that "Perhaps the nearest approach to a formulation of the general theory of relativity is that we observe only relations between physical entities" (LeShan, 1974). A large number of statements of this kind by both physicists and mystics (often indistinguishable as to which of the two persuasions was followed by the author) have been given elsewhere (LeShan, 1974).

Seen in this light, the clairvoyant reality is primarily a way of perceiving functional entities. We begin to see another reason for hypothesizing that paranormal events and functional entities are related.

Very well then, "when" is Uvani? It this a fruitful question? Does it help us to see further by asking? Let us try some answers. Uvani is "when" Eileen Garrett (or another medium) moves into a particular state of consciousness in the presence of a perceived need of a sitter. When she conceptualizes the world in a particular way (the clairvoyant reality) and, in this world-picture, conceptualizes Uvani as existing, he exists. Further, he is conceptualized as having certain characteristics. Under these conditions, a functional entity with these characteristics comes into existence and functions according to them.

Clearly, it is not as simple as this. For a functional entity with certain characteristics to come into existence (to be able to affect structural entities), a highly coherent *Weltbild*, a world-picture permitting these characteristics, must be fully believed in by the perceiving structural entity. This is as true for "the square root of minus one" as it is for Uvani. (It is useless to ask "what" the square root of minus one is. One can ask "when" it is and how it affects other functional and structural entities. We can get answers to these questions, but not the "what" question.) Not only must the *Weltbild* be accepted, the functional entity itself must be clearly conceptualized as potentially and actually existing. However, given these conditions of acceptance of a proper *Weltbild* for it and the belief in the functional entity, it can come into existence. Now we begin to see "when" Uvani is. Does this help us? To be helpful a concept must explain and help us to better organize the previously inexplicable and explicable data we have and also predict new data. Let us try to see if our concept here is fruitful.

It does seem to be able to explain the data we have. (This may be because it is so general, but, at this stage of the game, that is acceptable.) Certainly it explains why we have never been able to devise even a theoretical method for satisfactorily determining "what" a spirit control is. And it explains why we have never been able to devise instrumentation that would detect a spirit control directly. (If a telescope is focused on a wall a mile away, the *point of focus* exists. However, we cannot, even theoretically, detect it by any instrumentation in the wall or monitoring the wall. Yet it exists, and if properly conceived and perceived by a structural entity who has, for example, a cannon handy, can drastically affect the wall.)

In a curiously circular way, we explain Uvani's characteristics by saying that those are the characteristics he has. This procedure is invalid—at least since the end of the medieval period—when dealing with structural entities. It is the procedure we claim is valid when dealing with functional entities. The characteristics of "gravity" are those characteristics we give it when we wish to explain the tables of observations we make on solar phenomena. The functional entity "gravity" is a very useful one and enables us to explain old data and to predict new data, but its characteristics are explained by saying that those are its characteristics. To the question "what" is gravity we can only respond with a helpless shrug. The question "when" we can answer. We cannot detect it directly by sense-extending instrumentation, but we can certainly detect its effects.

A most dramatic demonstration of this concept and one of its implications has been given by Iris Owen and her associates. They devised a functional entity that was able to produce consistent paranormal phenomena. They started by writing an original story about an imaginary cavalier of King Charles I. This character, whom they called Philip, was married but in love with a gypsy girl. He installed her in the gatekeeper's lodge to his castle. His wife became jealous and accused the gypsy of witchcraft. Philip did not rise to her defense, and she was burned at the stake. In remorse he flung himself off the castle walls and died. After writing the story, the group sat around a table and tried to get Philip to communicate with them. Owen carefully coached the group in what she believed was the attitude toward reality that would make successful communication most likely. Presently an entity, which identified itself as Philip, began to manifest by loud rappings of the table—one for "yes" and two for "no." In answering questions the entity insisted that the story was true except for the fact that he had not been in love with the gypsy girl. It had only been a case of sexual infatuation.

Owen's table was an extremely strong and impressive one. She was an excellent experimenter, so she rotated the members of her group until every one of them had been absent on occasions when the table was active. Even when no members of the group were within three feet of the table (but a majority were in the room and working at the relationship) and in the full light in which they regularly worked, the raps were strong and clear. When recorded on an oscilloscope they produced a pattern with no "damping" effect that it did not seem possible to reproduce when the table was struck with a hand, foot or object that was tried. (I personally tried everything I could think of!)

And her group had hand-tailored a functional entity under the proper conditions and given it certain characteristics. It then had those characteristics and affected structural entities in the manner it had been designed to do. I believe *Conjuring Up Philip* (Owen with Sparrow, 1976) is one of the most significant books published in the field of psychical research for many years. In effect, Owen's group has given us a guidebook on how to "do" parapsychological research by designing the correct functional entities to accomplish those paranormal functions we wish to produce. Owen checked her research method by using other groups to devise other functional entities. One group using the same table-rapping technique got into regular and cogent communication with an entity identifying himself as "Santa Claus" and another identifying himself as the Easter Rabbit (who refused to reveal where he got the eggs)!

Let us now take the liberty of approaching Uvani in a roundabout method through another aspect of the paranormal, psychic healing. The evidence is clear enough. There is a type of "treatment" of physical problems that falls outside our presently accepted explicatory systems. The "healer" conceptualizes in a certain way. The "healee" responds (sometimes) with positive biological changes. Sometimes there is no apparent biological change. The healee may or may not know that the healer is "working" with him, may or may not believe in the whole idea, and may or may not be in the physical presence of the healer. Whatever is going on here?

I have elsewhere (LeShan, 1974) described the behavior that the serious healers believe is relevant to the healing. (Statements by healers

113

such as the Worralls, Ronald Beasley and Edgar Jackson indicate that they believe this analysis to be correct—see LeShan, 1974. Further, my doing these behaviors has produced positive healing results, and the same has been true of individuals to whom I and Joyce Goodrich taught them.) This set of behaviors consists of the healer accepting a world-picture in which the most important aspect of "things" is their interrelatedness and connectedness and in which isolation and separation are illusory. Accepting this fully—for at least the moment—to the degree that it completely fills the field of the healer's consciousness, he or she conceptualizes a special functional entity that fits organically and naturally into this metaphysic. This is that the healee is no longer a separate structural entity bound and isolated within the limits of his skin, but, with his or her uniqueness and individuality complete, the healee is a part of a functional entity that includes the entire cosmos or at least the healer and a good-sized chunk of the universe. For one moment, the healer's consciousness is completely filled with this concept. When the healing occurs, this is what the healer has been doing.

The healer has followed our rules for bringing into existence a functional entity: first by conceptualizing the proper metaphysical system and fully accepting its validity; second by conceptualizing a functional entity organically fitting into this world-picture and into the present situation as perceived with the use of this world-picture and accepting its validity. This newly brought-into-existence functional entity, perceived by the healer, and probably at some level by the healee, has effects on their structural entities. Have we begun to see some light directed into the paranormal aspects of psychic healing? The basic problem has been bridging the gap between healer and healee. Except when we are forced to it—as in the case of gravity—today we are acutely uncomfortable with anything that smacks of action-at-a-distance. It smells of the paranormal to us. In our normal world of space and time it *is* paranormal. Functional entities, however, are not limited by such criteria. And a functional entity that includes both healer and healee makes the gap between them disappear. Hey! Presto! Our psychic healing is no longer paranormal. What a convenient concept this one of the two kinds of entities is turning out to be!

However, it is all very well to present a theory about how the gap is bridged and to "explain" the effect of this on the structural entity of the healee. (I have done this last by hypothesizing that it places the healee in something closer to an "ideal organismic position" and thereby stimulates his or her own self-repair mechanisms to operate at a level closer to their potential: see LeShan, 1974.) Will this theory, however, predict new data? This is the nitty-gritty of a theory. Without this predictive ability all we have is interesting talk and pleasant games.

If healer and healee are included in a functional entity and the healer conceptualizes a functional entity that has positive therapeutic effects on the patient, the patient often responds with positive biological change. In the *Weltbild* the healer is using, a functional entity of this sort is perfectly reasonable. However, equally reasonable is a similar functional entity that has positive therapeutic effects on both the healer and the patient, on all parts of the entity, not just one part. If a functional entity of this sort is conceptualized, the therapeutic effects should be as great on both, and we should be able to perceive this. Now we begin to approach an experimental situation. Healers are well known for their inability to heal themselves. (There are one or two confusing cases, but basically the evidence is clear.) A change in the conceptualized functional entity should change this with no loss of healing effect on the healee. Certainly this is a testable prediction.

Other testable predictions can also be made now that we have the basic concept that functional entities can be hand-tailored so long as they fit organically into the *Weltbild* used. A wide variety of tests are now theoretically possible, of which the above is an example.

Conclusion

What I have described here is an approach to the problem of the paranormal. It is true that the normal laws of space and time cannot be violated by structural entities. (Which of the laws can be broken by a particular functional entity depends on its characteristics and the characteristics of the *Weltbild* within which it organically belongs.)

If we conceptualize the serious spirit controls as functional entities, the data we have become more understandable and it seems possible to predict new data.

Modern physics has used the concept I have called the "functional entity" to great advantage. The electron is a good example. The electron has, in Henry Margenau's words, "no determinate position" (Margenau, 1960, p. 326). James Jeans has written, "It is probably as meaningless to discuss how much room an electron takes up as it is to discuss how much room a fear, an anxiety or an uncertainty takes up" (Barnett, 1966, p. 28). Eddington has said "that an electron is not in one place, but is smeared over a probability distribution" (p. 50) and J. Robert Oppenheimer (1961) writes, "The electron cannot be objectified in a manner independent of the means chosen for observing or studying it" (p. 189). Clearly, we are not describing a structural entity in these terms. If science has found its electron, the square root of -1, gravity, and a host of other functional entities to be useful, it may be worthwhile to see if we can find it useful to conceptualize spirit controls in this way.

Appendix References

Barnett, Lincoln (1966). *The Universe and Dr. Einstein*. New York: William Morrow.

Broad, C. D. (1926). *Lectures in Psychical Research*. London: Routledge & Kegan Paul.

Eddington, Arthur S. (1958). *The Philosophy of Physical Science*. Ann Arbor: University of Michigan Press.

LeShan, Lawrence (1967). "The Vanished Man." *Journal of American Society for Psychical Research*, 132–42.

————. (1969 a). "Physicists and Mystics: Similarities in World Views." *Journal of Transpersonal Psychology*, 1, 1–19.

————. (1969 b). *Toward a General Theory of the Paranormal*. New York: Parapsychology Foundation.

————. (1974). *The Medium, the Mystic, and the Physicist*. New York: Viking.

Margenau, Henry (1960). *The Nature of Physical Reality*. New York: McGraw-Hill.

Oppenheimer, Robert. (1961). "Physics in the Contemporary World." In *Great Essays in Science*, ed. Gardner Murphy. New York: Washington Square Press.

Owen, Iris M., with Margaret Sparrow (1976). *Conjuring Up Philip: An Adventure in Psychokinesis*. New York: Harper & Row.

Progoff, Ira (1967). *Interviews with Eileen Garrett*. Unpublished manuscript at the Parapsychology Foundation.

Schrodinger, Erwin (1961). *Science and Humanism: Physics in Our Times*. Cambridge: Cambridge University Press.

Yeats, William Butler (1970). *A Vision*. New York: Collier.

Notes

CHAPTER 1: PSYCHIC RESEARCH
AND THE CONSISTENCY OF THE UNIVERSE

1. John G. Fuller, *The Ghost of Flight 401* (Berkeley, Calif.: Berkeley Publishing Company, 1976), 87.
2. Personal communication, 1969.
3. The best description of which I am aware of the various attempts to account for and explain the reports of psi is the superb work of John Beloff, *The Relentless Question: Reflections on the Paranormal* (Jefferson, N.C.: McFarland, 1990). A survey of the field that is very much worth reading is that of Robert M. Schoch and Logan Yonavjak, *The Parapsychology Revolution* (New York: Tarcher, 2008). Overall, when we try to determine what our observations of psi events "mean," we are left in somewhat the same position that authors Richard Smoley and Jay Kinney found themselves when they tried to deal with the problem of UFO sightings. They write, "All the current explanations—whether advanced by believers or by debunkers—are extremely tenuous. It is as absurd to write all of these sightings off as swamp gas or jetliners as it is to claim that they come from far off planets. As Jung said, 'We are only left with the conclusion that something is happening, but we don't know what'" (Richard Smoley and Jay Kinney, *Hidden Wisdom: A Guide to the Western Inner Traditions* [Wheaton, Ill.: Quest, 2006], 289.) Several years after the Carrington case occurred, I was discussing it with Mrs. Garrett. She said that she believed it was highly evidential, but she was not sure of what!

Notes

Chapter 2: What Do We Now Know About Psychic Phenomena?

1. Quoted by Walter Franklin Prince in Carl Murchison, *The Case For and Against Psychical Belief* (Worcester, Mass.: Clark University Press, 1927), 190.
2. We have seen the ability of "intention" to make small but significant changes in the number series emitted by a random-number generator. Do we, perhaps, have a glimpse of a new factor in evolution in the "random" variations in genetic structure that lead to changes in a species?
3. Quoted in Lawrence LeShan and Arthur Twitchell, eds., *The Mallorca Conference on Human Potentialities*, monograph (New York: American Society for Psychical Research, 1977), 172 ff.

Chapter 3: Normal and Paranormal Communication

Epigraph: C. W. E. Mundle, "Strange Facts in Search of a Theory," *Proceedings of the Society for Psychical Research* 56 (1973): 1–20. Mundle further suggests that in view of the anxiety and outrage produced in materialists at the idea of the existence of the "nonphysical," many modern people are as terrified at the idea of finding that they have a soul as medieval people would have been at the idea that they did not.

1. Gardner Murphy, "Psychical Research and Personality," *Proceedings of the Society for Psychical Research* 49 (1949–1952), 1–15, 6.
2. Ibid., 21–50, 33.
3. René Warcollier, *Mind to Mind* (New York: Collier, 1963).
4. John Beloff, "Trying to Make Sense out of the Paranormal," *Proceedings of the Society for Psychical Research* 56 (1975), 173-95, 177.
5. J. B. Rhine, "On Parapsychology and the Nature of Man," in *Dimensions of Mind,* ed. S. Hook (New York, Collier, 1960), 74–84, 75. Among others who have come to this conclusion—that "normal" and "paranormal" perceptions are the same in structure—are Ducasse; Thouless and Weisner; and Moncrief. See C. J. Ducasse, *Nature, Mind, and Death* (LaSalle, Ill.: Open Court, 1951); R. H. Thouless and B. P. Weisner, "The Psi Processes

in Normal and Paranormal Perception," *Proceedings of the Society for Psychical Research* 48 (1947): 180; and M. M. Moncrief, *The Clairvoyant Theory of Perception* (London: Faber and Faber, 1951).

6. Arthur S. Eddington, *Science and the Unseen World* (New York: Macmillan, 1937), 34.

7. Stuart Holroyd, *Psi and the Consciousness Explosion* (New York: Taplinger, 1977), 21.

8. E. W. Sinnott, *The Bridge of Life* (New York: Simon and Schuster, 1966), 168.

9. E. M. Weyer, "A Unit Concept of Consciousness," *Psychology Review* 17 (1910): 301–18.

10. C. E. M. Joad, book review, *The New Statesman and Nation* 23 (1948). Quoted in Jan Ehrenwald, *New Dimensions in Deep Analysis* (New York: Grune and Stratton, 1955), 213.

11. G. N. M. Tyrrell ("The Modus Operandi of Paranormal Cognition," *Proceedings of the Society for Psychical Research* 48 [1946]: 65–120) analyzed type B perceptions into two parts—a paranormal part and a "normal" part. He called them stage 1 and stage 2. He showed that stage 2 obeyed all the laws of the psychology of perception and regarded stage 1 as essentially unanalyzable. This is a somewhat more sophisticated approach than one generally finds in the field. However, Tyrrell did not take the next step and point out that normal cognition also has two stages, sensory-neural and conscious, and that different methods of analysis are needed for each. There are, of course, philosophers who claim to have demonstrated that consciousness either does not exist or is an illusion. I am, as I hope you are, perfectly clear that *my* consciousness exists. If you are a member of the group that believes consciousness is an illusion, I see no point in prolonging this discussion. At best we have two illusions talking to each other, and I cannot see the possibility of anything of benefit resulting from such an interchange. The second reason, although emotionally compelling, is less valid than it appears. As William James put it, "The first difference between the psychical researcher and the inexperienced person is that the former realizes the commonness and typicality of the phenomena, while the latter, less informed, thinks it so rare as to be unworthy of attention. I wish to go on record for the commonness." Quoted in Murchison, op. cit., 76.

CHAPTER 4: DESIGNING A
SCIENCE OF PARAPSYCHOLOGICAL RESEARCH

1. H. Margenau, *The Nature of Physical Reality* (New York: McGraw-Hill, 1950).

2. For example, the fact that perceived isolation leads to a breakdown of the usual self-perception, toward either chaos or an extremely painful self-orientation, has been widely reported. See, for example, the review in Darwyn E. Linder, *Psychological Dimensions of Social Interaction* (Reading, Mass.: Addison-Wesley, 1973), 9ff.

3. M. S. Olmstead, *The Small Group* (New York: Random House, 1950), 112.

4. D. Cartwright, "The Nature of Group Cohesiveness," in *Group Dynamics*, 3rd ed., eds. D. Cartwright and Alvin Zander (New York: Harper, 1968), 91–101.

5. Carl Sargent, personal communication, April 1978. The hypothesis that psi occurrences are more frequent between people who like each other than between people who do not is far from a new idea in the field. We are concerned here more with a general system for developing testable hypotheses than with whether these hypotheses are old or new.

6. Robert F. Bales, *Interaction Process Analysis: A Method for the Study of Small Groups* (Reading, Mass.: Addison-Wesley, 1950).

7. "There is one area where the conclusions drawn from ESP studies are largely consistent with what we have learned from other topics. This common area deals with the personality dynamics of ESP success and failure." Gertrude R. Schmeidler and Robert A. McConnell, *ESP and Personality Patterns* (New Haven, Conn.: Yale University Press, 1958), 4.

8. It is no longer necessary to point out that babies raised by Parisians grow up with the identity and self-awareness of French city dwellers, and that the same relationship is true in Eskimo and Yorkshire homes: "A society without members or individuals without socialization cannot exist. Although they can be analyzed separately, the two are indistinguishable in nature." Reece McGee, *Points of Departure: Basic Concepts in Sociology* (Hinsdale, Ill.: Dryden Press, 1973), 99.

9. Olmstead, op. cit.

10. Erik Erikson, "Identity and Uprootedness in Our Time," in *Varieties of Modern Social Theory*, Hendrik Marinus Ruitenbeek (New York: Dutton, 1963), 55–68.

11. In the language used here, a "gestalt" is a set of interrelated observables in the same sense in which a "state" of a physical system is described as a combination of observables.

12. Cassirer, *Philosophy of Symbolic Forms; Language and the Myth* (New York: Harper and Row, 1940).

13. Elizabeth Barrett Browning, *Sonnets from the Portuguese,* no. 43.

14. These seminars are being taught at this time by Dr. Joyce Goodrich (CRTP@mindspring.com) and Dr. Mary Bobis (somedee@aol.com).

15. Lawrence LeShan, *The Dilemma of Psychology* (New York: Helios, 2002).

16. Precognition may be difficult for most of us to accept, but that it violates any fundamental concepts of modern science is very dubious: "All philosophers imagine that causation is one of the fundamental axioms of science, yet oddly enough, in advanced sciences the word 'cause' never occurs. . . . The law of causality, I believe, is a relic of a bygone age, surviving, like the monarchy, only because it is erroneously supposed to do no harm." Bertrand Russell (quoted in Dean Radin, "Time-Reversed Human Experience: Experimental Evidence and Implications" (unpublished manuscript, 2000, Esalen draft); "The implications [of the existence of precognition] are heresies of the first order. But I believe that if the scientific evidence continues to compound, then the accusation of heresy is an inescapable conclusion that we will eventually have to face. I also believe that the implications of all this are sufficiently remote from engrained ways of thinking that the first reaction to this work will be confidence that it is wrong. The second reaction will be horror that it may be right. The third will be reassurance that it is obvious." Radin, "Time-Reversed Human Experience." (This is a careful and detached meta-analysis of the experimental evidence in the study of precognition. If you have the courage to examine your belief systems in this area, or simply wish to know what you are talking about when you discuss it, I suggest reading it.) F. C. S. Schiller wrote that the first canon of psychical research is that *nothing is incredible if the evidence for it is good enough.* Each person evaluating this field must decide whether or not he or she accepts this statement; or, if he or she is bringing along an already made-up mind about what is the limit of the universe, what can be accepted as possible and what is the "boggle point" (that point at which the mind "boggles" and refuses to go further). Nearly all of us have unconsciously decided that the limits of our vision are the limits of the universe. We seem to have a remarkable ability to ignore

the simple truth that something either occurred or it did not, and that if an impossible fact occurred that that is important, that it forever alters our conviction of what is impossible and thereby changes the definition of the universe and the human condition.

CHAPTER 5: PSI AND ALTERED STATES OF CONSCIOUSNESS

1. Henry Margenau, *The Nature of Physical Reality* (New York: McGraw-Hill, 1950), 194.
2. Quoted in John G. Fuller, *The Ghost of Flight 401* (Berkeley, Calif.: Berkeley Publishing Company, 1976), 87.
3. This paragraph is a paraphrase of some comments of P. W. Bridgman in his *Logic of Modern Physics* (New York: Macmillan, 1960), 46. He quotes Herman Feigl: "Science is truth until further notice."
4. Wilhelm Windelband, *An Introduction to Philosophy*, trans. Joseph McCabe (New York: Henry Holt), 14. (Original publication 1914)

CHAPTER 6: THE NEXT STEP:
IMPLICATIONS OF THE NEW SCIENCE

1. Allan Angoff, *Eileen Garrett and the World beyond the Senses* (New York: William Morrow, 1974).
2. Lawrence LeShan and Arthur Twitchell, eds., *The Mallorca Conference on Human Priorities*, monograph (New York: American Society for Psychical Research, 2008), 168.
3. Elisabeth L. Mayer, *Extraordinary Knowing* (New York: Bantam, 2007).
4. William McDougall, "Psychical Research in a University Setting," in Carl Murchison, ed., *The Case for and Against Psychical Belief* (Worcester, Mass.: Clark University Press, 1927), 160.
5. Quoted in Murchison, *Psychical Belief,* 180, 160.
6. William Oliver Stevens, *Psychics and Common Sense* (New York: Dutton, 1955), 9.
7. Quoted in Stevens, *Psychics and Common Sense.*
8. C. D. Broad, *Lectures in Psychical Research* (London: Routledge and Kegan Paul, 1962), 6.

9. The deleted material consists of general statements, some personality descriptions, and some concrete statements that would be potentially hurtful to the individuals concerned. The entire annotated record is on file at the Parapsychology Foundation and is available to qualified researchers.
10. Based on letters and notes of telephone conversations with Mrs. B.
11. Jules Eisenbud, "The Problem of Resistance to Psi Phenomena." Dinner Address to the Ninth Annual Convention of the Parapsychological Association, New York City, September 8–10, 1966. *Proceedings of the Parapsychological Association* 3 (1969).

Chapter 7: What Dare I Hope?

1. The segment of reality necessary for the survival of a species (its "alpha" segment) is the segment revealed by its sensory array. These segments can differ widely. The species must act as if its senses revealed the true nature of reality or it becomes extinct. In this sense, reality is "species-specific."
2. See, for example, W. R. Inge: "All the great Western mystics have been energetic and influential, and their business capacity is specially noted in a curiously large number of cases." Quoted in Rudolph Otto, *Mysticism East and West: A Comparative Analysis of the Nature of Mysticism* (New York: Meridian, 1975), 67.

Index

Index

Related Quest Titles

Becoming a Practical Mystic, by Jacquelyn Small
Head and Heart, by Victor Mansfield
The Practice of Dream Healing, by Edward Tick
Our Psychic Sense, by Phoebe Bendit, with Laurence Bendit
The Radiant Child, by Thomas Armstrong
Science and the Sacred, by Ravi Ravindra
Spiritual Healing, by Dora van Gelder Kunz
The Visionary Window, by Amit Goswami

Praise for Lawrence LeShan's

A New Science of the Paranormal

"Drawing on a lifetime of research into the further reaches of consciousness, Lawrence LeShan brilliantly draws the outlines of a wider science and a deeper worldview. Compulsory reading, especially for professional psychologists and philosophers."

—David Lorimer,
Program Director, Scientific and Medical Network

"Larry LeShan's work has been of seminal importance to healers and parapsychologists for over thirty years. His compassion, curiosity, and vision have expanded our understanding of unity consciousness and psychic abilities. Thank you, Larry."

—Jane Katra, Ph.D.,
author of *Miracles of Mind* and *The Heart of the Mind*